Learning to Learn
with Integrative
Learning Technologies
(ILT)

A Practical Guide for Academic Success

Learning to Learn with Integrative Learning Technologies (ILT)

A Practical Guide for Academic Success

Anastasia Kitsantas, PhD
George Mason University

Nada Dabbagh, PhD
George Mason University

INFORMATION AGE PUBLISHING, INC.
Charlotte, NC • www.infoagepub.com

Library of Congress Cataloging-in-Publication Data

Kitsantas, Anastasia.
  Learning to learn with integrative learning technologies (ILT) : a
practical guide for academic success / Anastasia Kitsantas, Nada Dabbagh.
      p. cm.
  Includes bibliographical references.
  ISBN 978-1-60752-302-4 (pbk.) – ISBN 978-1-60752-303-1 (hardcover) –
ISBN 978-1-60752-304-8 (e-book)
1. Education, Higher–Computer-assisted instruction. 2. Educational
technology. 3. Study skills. I. Dabbagh, Nada. II. Title.
  LB2395.7.K57 2009
  378.1'7344678–dc22

                                                        2009039167

Printed in the United States of America

Contents

Preface

After more than a decade of researching how to support student self-regulation with technology in online and distributed learning contexts, *Learning to Learn with Integrative Learning Technologies (ILT): A Practical Guide for Academic Success,* has been written to facilitate college students' academic success by fostering self-regulated learning or "learning to learn" through the use of Integrative Learning Technologies (ILT). In this book we define ILT as a dynamic collection or aggregation of Web tools, software applications, and mobile technologies that integrate technological and pedagogical features and affordances of the Internet and the World Wide Web to facilitate the design, development, delivery, and management of online and distributed learning. The prevalence of course- and learning-management systems in higher education warranted a careful analysis of the influence of such systems on student learning based on theory, research, and practice.

This book provides an overview of the theory of self-regulation from a social cognitive perspective and describes how the principles and processes of this theory can be applied through the design of engaging instructional and learning activities using ILT. The process of interrelating technology and self-regulated learning, which is the focus of this book, enables the college instructor, online instructor, instructional developer, or educator to envision, plan for, and implement customized instructional designs that foster learning to learn and motivate students to take ownership of their own learning.

This book as a practical guide also provides explicit strategies and subject-matter-specific examples of how college faculty and instructors can draw on the pedagogical and technological features of ILT to promote or foster self-regulated learning and motivation. This is important particularly in online and blended college freshman courses in which students need the most support in order to succeed (e.g., large introductory courses and remedial mathematics or English courses). In addition, this book can be used in introductory college courses that address study skills development for freshmen. College instructors will be able to use this book to design learning tasks and assignments that foster study skills using ILT.

Specifically, instructors will be able to use ILT to design learning activities that support and promote the following student self-regulatory processes:

- goals
- use of appropriate task strategies
- self-monitoring and self-evaluation
- time management
- help-seeking behavior
- motivation and affect.

Each of the chapters in this book integrates the following components:

- Scenarios: A scenario related to issues that college instructors face in educating students to become proactive learners is provided. The scenarios are subject-matter-specific and address real situations that instructors face when teaching remedial and introductory college courses.
- Self-regulation and motivation research: A review of the influence of self-regulation and motivation processes on student learning and performance is provided.
- Research on ILT: A review of the influence of ILT on teaching and learning overall and on the specific self-regulatory processes is provided. This review includes traditional learning technologies such as course- and learning-management systems, as well as more current Web 2.0 technologies and social software.
- ILT tools and features: A description of the different ILT tools and features and the types of self-regulatory processes they support is provided. Tables and figures are included depicting the alignment between the specific features of ILT and self-regulatory processes.
- Instructional application: A self-regulatory training model to demonstrate how the instructor can, in a step-by-step manner, use ILT to promote student self-regulation and motivation is presented.

This book differs from other books related to study skills in several distinct ways. First, it has been written by experts in two distinct fields, Educational Psychology and Instructional Technology. This unique collaboration combines knowledge and research related to self-regulated learning and instructional technology generating new implications for practice. Second, it allows for a broader approach to the enhancement of learning by informing instructors how to use self-regulatory processes to help students maximize their academic potential and learn how to become independent learners. Finally, this book targets primarily undergraduate students enrolled in remedial or large introductory courses who need the most support to succeed.

Given the emphasis on retention of freshmen as a measure of institutional effectiveness, the focus on student success, and the increasing use of ILT in higher-education, we believe that this book fulfills a dire need in the literature on the integration of technology and self-regulated learning, or learning to learn.

Acknowledgments

We would like to dedicate this book to our husbands Steve and Omar and our children Yanna, and Bassel and Kareem. In addition, numerous students enrolled in the Educational Psychology and Instructional Technology programs at George Mason University have assisted with the completion of this book. We would like to thank Karen Dunn, Faye Huie, and Swetambari Shah.

1

Introduction to Learning How to Learn

Contents

Learning to Learn with Integrative Learning Technologies, pages 1–17
Copyright © 2010 by Information Age Publishing
All rights of reproduction in any form reserved.

1

Scenario

> *Children have to be educated, but they have also to be left to educate themselves.*
> —Abbé Dimnet, *Art of Thinking* (1928)

Ellen is a college instructor teaching a remedial mathematics course. She has 70 college freshmen enrolled in the class. It is the beginning of the semester and she is facing many challenges. These challenges stem primarily from the students' lack of study skills and Ellen's inability to reach each student face-to-face. Specifically, previous experience has taught Ellen that these students are uninterested in the course content, have low self-efficacy beliefs to achieve the course objectives, and generally lack motivation.

In addition, due to previous failures in math courses, these students have adopted a variety of maladaptive behaviors such as ineffective strategies and outcome self-monitoring, rather than strategic/adaptive monitoring to use during the learning process. For these reasons, these students are likely to focus on outcomes rather than on processes and hence lack the ability to set effective goals. Furthermore, these students have difficulty developing a focused plan for approaching the course material and are likely to attribute failure to lack of ability, rather than strategy use, and have negative self-reactions. Finally, these students avoid seeking help, which perpetuates these issues. Ellen realizes that in order to help these students succeed in the course, she will need to develop specific instructional plans based on her knowledge of the "learning how to learn" approach. Her goal is to teach students how to become proactive, responsible, self-regulated learners.

What Is Self-Regulated Learning?

It is very common for instructors who, like Ellen, teach large freshmen remedial courses in math and English, to encounter students who lack self-regulatory skills. Given that there is no one strategy that works for every individual in every learning context, self-regulatory skills can help the learner identify what he or she knows, what he or she does not know, and what he or she is trying to accomplish in an area of interest. Self-regulatory skills help students become responsible for their own learning, including setting appropriate goals for themselves, monitoring and evaluating their learning, using time effectively, and staying motivated. The development of students' self-regulatory skills has been a major focus of research on self-regulated learning (see chapters in edited books by Boekaerts, Pintrich, & Zeidner, 2000; Schunk & Zimmerman, 2008; Zimmerman, 2008). Thus, the question is, What is self-regulated learning?

Self-regulated learning refers to goal-oriented actions that an individual uses to acquire knowledge and skill without reliance on others (i.e., teachers, parents, or peers). A plethora of research studies shows that low-achieving college students are deficient or display fewer self-regulatory strategies relative to high-achieving students. However, these strategies or skills can be taught to low-achieving students to enhance learning and performance. Self-regulation instruction has been shown to be effective within a wide range of ages and cultures and has been effectively applied across domains such as academic learning, sports training, health functioning, and realms of expert performance (Kitsantas & Zimmerman, 1998; Schunk & Zimmerman, 1998; Zimmerman & Kitsantas, 1999). The importance of adaptive use of self-regulatory strategies is critical at the post-secondary level due to the demands of higher-level thinking and the focus on independent learning (Zimmerman, 2000). Therefore it is our contention that teaching college students to self-regulate their learning may serve to form a very powerful educational tool in creating an innovative educational reform initiative. We want to share a vision of learning that liberates educators and learners from the constraints of many traditional learning theories that explain academic achievement as a function of innate learner abilities or social-environmental backgrounds. By involving instructors in training on self-regulated learning, instructors can shift from an authoritarian role to that of a learning consultant who encourages students to independently self-reflect and adjust their efforts.

Self-regulation from a social cognitive view is unique because it involves the simultaneous interplay of several aspects of student learning including cognitive, motivational, affective, and contextual (Pintrich, 2004, Zimmerman, 2000). Based on Bandura's (1986) reciprocal determinism theory which posits that an individual's behavior involves a reciprocal interaction among the individual, the environment, and behavior, Zimmerman (2000) suggests self-regulatory functioning is the result of the interaction among behavioral (e.g., the ability to adjust one's behavioral learning processes such as study strategies), environmental (e.g., the ability to adjust environmental factors), and covert (e.g., the ability to monitor and adjust one's affective and cognitive states) processes. One key component of Zimmerman's model is the cyclical and interactive nature of all these processes.

Successful self-regulation involves constantly adjusting affect, behaviors, and cognitions based on the evaluative feedback from each of the three components until optimal levels of performance are achieved. It should be also noted that learners must be motivated to use self-regulated learning strategies. A powerful form of motivation is self-efficacy beliefs which refer to the degree to which a learner feels capable of mastering a specific task. In the next section, we define the specific processes of self-regulated learning and we provide suggestions on how Ellen, the instructor depicted in the chapter scenario, could help her students develop self-regulation skills to succeed in math related courses.

What Are Self-Regulatory Processes?

Self-regulatory processes such as goal setting, self-monitoring and self-evaluating are utilized by the learner to produce desired outcomes. There is ample research evidence to support the role of self-regulatory processes in optimal learning and performance (Ertmer, & Newby, 1996; Zimmerman, 2000). In fact, the self-regulation perspective presumes that these processes mediate the relationship between characteristics of the context and the student, and the learning outcomes (Pintrich, 2004, Zimmerman 2008). In this book, we will review the following self-regulation processes that have emerged during previous investigations of optimal performance in a variety of domains: (a) goal setting, (b) task strategies, (c) self-monitoring, (d) self-evaluation, (e) time management, and (f) help seeking. Table 1.1 provides the definitions of these processes and related instructional examples. It also differentiates how low- versus high-achieving individuals approach these processes.

Goal Setting

Goal setting involves the learner setting a standard or criterion for performance and is considered to be a powerful learning and motivational process (Zimmerman, 2000). Research on goal setting shows that specific, proximal, short-term, challenging but attainable, and process- rather than outcome-oriented goals lead to higher levels of academic attainment, particularly for novice learners. Process goals focus on methods to achieve a goal, whereas performance outcome goals focus on the end product (Zimmerman, 2008; Zimmerman & Kitsantas, 1999). The students that Ellen is teaching in the large remedial math class will need guidance in setting specific, short-term, process-oriented goals that provide learners with incremental and attainable steps to solve a math problem. This is critical in light of the previous failures that these students have had in math classes.

TABLE 1.1 Self-Regulatory Processes for Low- and High-Achieving Students and Instructional Support

Self-regulatory process	Definition	Students		Instructional support examples for the student
		Low-achieving	High-achieving	
Goal Setting	• A standard or criterion set by the learner	Vague goals Outcome goals Easy goals	Specific goals Process goals Challenging goals	• Help the learner set short-term, specific, process-oriented goals
Task Strategies	• Specific strategies which assist the learner to reduce a task to its essential features and then reorganize these features into a meaningful whole	Adoption of ineffective strategies	Initiate learning tasks Technique oriented Select appropriate strategies according to task demands Develop, modify, transfer strategies to new contexts	• Help the learner analyze the task and choose the appropriate strategies • Help the learner break the task into smaller components • Provide the learner with a list of strategies • Assist the learner in recognizing which strategies are effective and/or ineffective in achieving his or her goals
Self-Monitoring	• A process that learners use to keep track of their learning progress	Outcome monitoring	Process monitoring	• Assist the learner to assess both processes and outcomes with specific, personalized feedback • Instruct the learner how to keep records and graph results to view and monitor his or her goal progress

(continued)

TABLE 1.1 Self-Regulatory Processes for Low- and High-Achieving Students and Instructional Support (continued)

Self-regulatory process	Definition	Students		Instructional support examples for the student
		Low-achieving	High-achieving	
Self-Evaluating	• Evaluation of an *outcome* of learning or performance against a set standard or criterion	Avoid self-evaluation	Frequent engagement in self-evaluation	• Assist the learner to use self-monitored outcomes to evaluate his or her performance outcomes against his or her goals • Help the learner identify deficits and learning gaps
Time Management	• Use of planning for sequencing, allocating time, and completing activities	Lack self-management skills	Seek to learn how to plan their time effectively	• Teach the learner to create calendars to plan for exams and projects over time and in advance • Help the learner break the material into smaller sections for studying to avoid procrastination • Teach the learner to prioritize activities and to set realistic time limits for the completion of tasks
Help Seeking	• Student-initiated efforts to obtain information from social and nonsocial sources	Avoid seeking help	Seek help from social and nonsocial sources	• Facilitate help seeking by promoting the use of study groups and collaborative learning • Create nonthreatening learning environments

Ellen should also provide her students with feedback (i.e., verbal encouragement) that is related to their progress toward an academic goal over the course of the semester. These actions will help the students develop greater self-efficacy beliefs, which will have a positive effect on their learning. Chapter 4 describes goal setting as a process of self-regulated learning in detail.

Task Strategies

Task strategies refer to analyzing tasks and identifying methods for learning various parts of a task (Zimmerman, 2000, Zimmerman, Bonner, & Kovach, 1996). Many unsuccessful learners have adopted strategies that are ineffective. Such students need to be taught when certain strategies should be used, why they are used, and how to use them to achieve certain goals. Not all strategies will be effective across different contexts and tasks. Therefore, in order for students to effectively use a task strategy to help them learn, students must first be able to identify which strategies would be the most helpful in their situation. For an instructor such as Ellen, identification of ineffective strategies will be an important first step in helping students replace ineffective strategies with more effective ones. She will need to offer students a variety of strategies that promote self-regulated learning behaviors and teach her students to match strategies to their learning goals. Ellen will want to suggest strategies that encourage deep, reflective processing (e.g., visualization, concept mapping, mnemonics). This is in contrast to the use of surface strategies such as repeated memorization techniques, which rarely promote meaningful learning.

However, showing students how to use the strategies will not be helpful if they do not choose to use them on their own while studying independently. Therefore, in addition to teaching students the strategies, Ellen should also make the benefits of using such strategies explicit. This instructional approach will encourage and motivate students to use the learned strategies with other learning tasks. Chapter 5 describes task strategies as a process of self-regulated learning in detail.

Self-Monitoring

Self-monitoring involves the intentional observation of one's behavior. Self-monitoring is a cognitive process that learners use to assess their learning progress in relation to goals. In addition, self-monitoring generates feedback that can promote and guide future action and it is considered to be a key component of self-regulatory behavior (Zimmerman, 2000). For example, students who self-monitor initiate a self-reflective process that involves all aspects of the learner and the learning environment in which learning occurs. The feedback that results from this process will determine goal commitment. As the instructor, Ellen will need to provide instruction that encourages continual self-monitoring in her students. Examples of self-monitoring could be providing students with a form or a chart that gives them a visual representation of the progress they are making toward achieving the goal. In turn, self-monitoring can help Ellen's students feel that they have control over the learning process, which can facilitate intrinsic motivation and increase their perceived ability to cope with and persist through difficult tasks. Additionally, providing students with a chart to record or graph their progress will encourage them to reflect on the quality of their own work and what strategies need to be used to improve their work. Possible questions that Ellen could ask students to use to promote their use of self-monitoring include, Have I followed the appropriate steps? and, Am I making progress? Chapter 6 describes self-monitoring as a process of self-regulated learning in detail.

Self-Evaluation

Self-evaluation involves the learner evaluating an outcome of learning or performance against a set standard or criterion. It may also involve setting individual standards by the learner to use for self-judgment. It is important to distinguish self-evaluation from self-monitoring. Self-evaluation differs from self-monitoring in the sense that evaluation involves a comparison between performance and a standard or outcome criterion, whereas self-monitoring is limited to the tracking and recording of one's performance without comparing effort to outcome. Self-regulated students self-evaluate by comparing performance to desired outcomes, identifying gaps in their learning, and initiating efforts to correct performance gaps. This is in contrast to students who lack the ability to self-regulate and may therefore have difficulty monitoring and detecting failure if they do not understand how to evaluate their learning (Zimmerman, 2000). Therefore, Ellen will need to assist her students to accurately self-evaluate their work and encourage them to self-evaluate based on their degree of mastery, rather than comparing their performance to that of other students. In addition, Ellen should provide assignment evaluation criteria to help her students check their progress during assignment completion and evaluation feedback based on the same criteria. This technique could promote student self-evaluation during the learning process as well as after the completion of assignments (Ley & Young, 2001). Chapter 6 describes in detail self-evaluation as a process of self-regulated learning.

Time Management

Time management involves the learner's use of planning for sequencing, allocating time, and completing activities. It can also entail breaking study material into manageable pieces. Time management is a topic that has been widely studied in a variety of contexts and has emerged as a strong predictor of academic success (Loomis, 2000) as well as an anticipatory strategy that can prompt the use of other self-regulatory strategies (Zimmerman, Greenberg, & Weinstein, 1994). In addition, information gleaned from case studies of students in online learning environments indicates that time management skills are crucial for planning course activities and coordinating scheduling demands (Whipp & Chiarelli, 2004).

Effective time management has two main components—the allocation of adequate time for learning and accurate assessment of the actual use of the time allocated. For example, a student may allocate adequate time for learning through the appropriate scheduling of activities, the setting of priorities and goals, and by creating checklists of completed tasks. However, if the student does not accurately assess the quality of his or her learning time, performance can suffer. Toward this end, Ellen will want to teach her students to ask themselves questions related to their study time and learning. These questions could include, How well am I spending my time on this task?, Have I been using my study time wisely? and How might I study better? Additionally, Ellen can use different time management strategies derived from research (e.g., Cennamo, Ross, & Rogers, 2002; Terry & Doolittle, 2006) to help students manage the demands of course-related activities. Examples of these strategies include clearly communicating deadlines and test dates and encouraging students to create individualized lists of tasks they need to accomplish, as well as subtasks within the larger tasks with details on when each task is due. Chapter 7 describes time management as a process of self-regulated learning in detail.

Help Seeking

Help seeking is defined as student-initiated efforts to obtain information from social and nonsocial sources. Research evidence shows that seeking needed assistance from social and nonsocial sources is an important process that highly correlates with student achievement (Ames, 1983; Karabenick & Knapp, 1988; Kitsantas & Chow, 2007). In regard to the scenario in this chapter, Ellen should encourage students to become adaptive help seekers—that is, students should be trained to seek help when they do not understand or are unable to comprehend a complex concept on their own. Particularly, Ellen should focus on low-achieving students, who are less likely to initiate help-seeking strategies than their high-achieving classmates. Low-achieving students should be encouraged to ask for assistance and taught how to seek help selectively by knowing how and what to ask. No matter what questions students ask, they should not be ridiculed or censured, either of which could discourage students' future attempts to ask for help. Chapter 8 describes help seeking as a process of self-regulated learning in detail.

How Are Self-Regulatory Processes Related? Self-Empowering Cycles of Learning

We have described the major self-regulatory processes that learners can use to improve their learning. These processes can be used to create self-empowering cycles of learning and have been integrated in a three-phase conceptual model of self-regulated learning (Zimmerman, 2000, 2008), (see Figure 1.1).

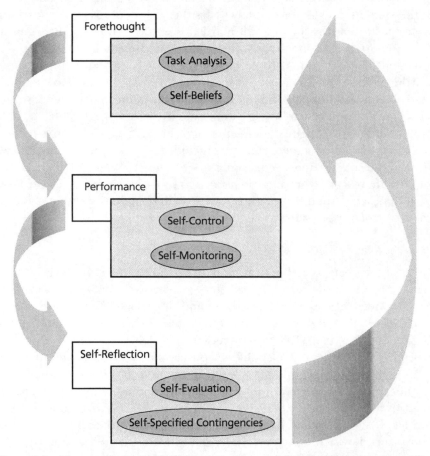

Figure 1.1   Zimmerman's (2000, 2008) three-phase model of self-regulated learning.

The first phase of the model, the forethought phase, includes two distinct subcategories: task analysis and self-beliefs. This preliminary phase involves the cognitive processes that the learner undertakes prior to initiating an activity. The second phase, the performance phase, represents the action phase, which includes the strategies that the learner employs to actually perform the activity. The performance phase includes the two subcategories of self-control and self-monitoring. The learner in this phase uses strategic processes such as self-instruction and environmental structuring and engages in self-observation via metacognitive monitoring or record keeping, focusing on specific aspects of his or her performance. The final phase, self-reflection, includes the subcategories of self-evaluation and self-specified contingencies. It is within this phase that the learner evaluates his or her performance, usually in comparison to a personal or self-imposed standard or a goal. These evaluations then proceed to influence the forethought phase of subsequent efforts. Thus, the three phases of this model are cyclically interrelated in a self-oriented system of feedback. The student continues to adjust self-regulated strategies to meet current or new demands to optimize learning. This cycle of learning promotes individual empowerment, in part because it reinforces the beliefs of the individual in his or her ability to effectively control aspects of the learning experience toward a desired outcome.

Supporting College Students' Use of Self-Regulatory Processes

Numerous research studies show that self-regulation plays a critical role in an individual's academic performance (Zimmerman, 2000, 2008; Zimmerman & Kitsantas, 1999). In fact, student inability to self-regulate learning behaviors is a crucial reason for academic learning difficulties (Zimmerman & Schunk, 2008). On the other hand, students who are effective self-regulators tend to possess and utilize motivation, affective components, and appropriate strategies to achieve their academic goals. These students also self-evaluate their performance and subsequently adapt future behavior accordingly (Zimmerman, 2000).

Researchers have argued that teaching students self-regulatory strategies should be dependent on specific, contextual needs (Hofer, Yu, & Pintrich, 1998). Hofer et al. (1998) suggest that although it may be relatively simple to discuss with college freshmen students the nature of self-regulatory strategies, it may be more difficult to convince students to replace previously effective strategies with more effective ones as they transition into college from high school where different demands are placed on the learner. Teaching college students to become adaptive as they select strategies to accomplish new goals is critical in helping them become proactive learners.

Furthermore, some studies show that teaching one specific strategy to college students impeded their ability to generalize the strategy use across different domains, while other studies have shown that teaching too many strategies was problematic because students may have difficulty distinguishing among the different strategies (Hattie, Biggs, & Purdie, 1996). Issues to consider when teaching students how to self-regulate include the scope (How many strategies should be focused on?), content (Does the course require domain-specific strategies, or is it a "learning to learn" course?), and time frame (When does the class end; when is the next test?). In addition, in order to promote successful implementation of strategies, the learner must be motivated and self-efficacious in his or her ability to utilize these strategies appropriately to achieve set goals. College instructors should provide students with strategies that are powerful enough to produce some success, consequently fueling student motivation to continue pursuing the task.

For example, in the chapter scenario, the instructor should use specific and contextualized strategies to ensure the success of low-achieving students. To this end, Ellen will need to teach her students what the specific strategies are, how to use them, and when and why to use these strategies based on the math concept they are trying to master. This instructional approach can ensure that students utilize specific and appropriate strategies to accomplish their course goals. Additionally, encouraging students to recognize and celebrate small successes can build their self-efficacy beliefs and decrease performance-related anxiety.

Developing Self-Regulatory Competence and Motivation Through Social Cognitive Training: Describing the Role of the Instructor

Based on extensive research, learners' acquisition of new skills (e.g., writing a research paper, solving a math problem) becomes self-regulated in four sequential phases: observation, emulation, self-control, and self-regulation (Kitsantas, Zimmerman, & Cleary, 2000; Zimmerman, 2000). The first two phases (observation and emulation) focus on social learning experiences that prepare learners to attain higher levels of skill on their own.

An observation level of skill is achieved when modeling experiences provide a learner with a clear image of how a skill should be performed, such as when a learner is able to discriminate the main steps of a first-degree math equation by observing the performance of an expert instructor. Modeling is the process through which information is conveyed from the expert to the observer. A learner observes a model's actions, hears their descriptions, and observes their consequences. A learner's motivation in this phase is enhanced vicariously by observing rewards attained by the model or the expert instructor.

In the emulation phase, a learner acquires experiences in close proximity to modeling and from social feedback. Emulation is the process by which information is gained from efforts to reenact the performance of an expert model. Learners have achieved this level of competence when they emulate the general form of the modeled skill, such as following the steps in solving the first-degree equation. These emulative performance experiences provide learners with social feedback to refine their performance and to develop standards of correct performance that are essential for higher levels of learning. Social feedback is a primary source of motivation for learners in this phase.

In the self-control phase of Zimmerman and colleagues' model, students learn from self-directed practice to achieve automaticity of the basic components of the task. To attain this level of proficiency, students must compare their practice efforts with personal standards acquired previously from an expert's performance. Automaticity is attained most readily when learners focus on processes (or techniques) rather than on outcomes. A primary source of motivation in this phase is the students' self-reactions (e.g., satisfaction with performance), stemming from matching or surpassing process-oriented standards.

In the self-regulation phase of the training model, students learn to adapt their performance to changes in internal and external conditions. To accomplish this, students must shift their attention from modeled processes to performance outcomes. For example, writers can self-monitor to determine which strategies produce the best outcome. Two primary sources of motivation in this phase are self-efficacy beliefs and intrinsic interest in the skill. Table 1.2 provides brief descriptions of the four phases of this training model and examples of how an instructor can use them to foster student self-regulation.

This training model of self-regulation has been tested with various learning tasks and the results show that it is a powerful tool in helping students become self-regulated learners. However, can this model be implemented in online or blended contexts? This is an important question because of the rising number of courses delivered online and the high rates of student attrition in such courses. The development and nurturing of self-regulatory

TABLE 1.2   Self-Regulatory Training and Instructional Examples

Phases of self-regulation training	Definition	Instructional examples
Observation	• Learner observes the instructor or a skilled peer perform a task • Learner begins to discriminate the correct strategies for completing the task	• Model step-by-step how to perform a particular task • Convey specific cognitive and performance techniques needed to perform the task • Provide repeated observations rather than a single exposure
Emulation	• Learner emulates the procedure as modeled by the instructor	• Encourage and support the learner by providing positive feedback • Reduce learner support gradually to ensure that the learner takes on more responsibility as he or she increases in skill proficiency
Self-Control	• Learner begins to practice the task without the use of models • Learner focuses on process-oriented goals	• Instruct learner to focus on mastering the steps • Teach learner to engage in self-monitoring by providing charts
Self-Regulation	• Learner shifts attention to outcome goals	• Guide learner when errors occur

processes are particularly needed in online or blended courses since students are responsible for much of their own learning in these contexts. This is in contrast to the highly structured classroom environments that students experience in high school, which are typically characterized by continual instructor support and guidance throughout the learning process. For example, the need to monitor comprehension in these learning contexts is important, as is the need to promote collaborative learning among students. In addition, students in online learning environments need training to use tools in order to set appropriate goals and accurately self-observe and assess their academic progress. Online learning technologies can provide students with immediate feedback related to their performance, which can serve to facilitate the learning process.

Our aim in this book is to demonstrate how instructors can support self-regulated learning in online or blended learning contexts. In Chapter 2, we describe the learning technologies available for instructors to support and facilitate online learning. We refer to these technologies as Integrative Learning Technologies (ILT). In Chapter 3, we align the self-regulated processes discussed in this chapter to ILT categories and features in order to demonstrate how instructors can use ILT to support student self-regulated learning in general. In subsequent chapters (4–7), we address each self-regulatory process independently and use the self-regulated training model presented in Table 1.2 to demonstrate how instructors can use ILT to support and promote student use of the specific self-regulatory process. Finally, in Chapter 9 we discuss motivation, affect, and learning communities, and in Chapter 10, we focus on new approaches to ILT.

Conclusion

This chapter provided an overview of the theory of self-regulation and its processes (e.g., goal setting, task strategies, self-monitoring, self-evaluation) and described how these processes are conceptually related in a three-phase (forethought, performance, and self-reflection) cyclical model. Research on self-regulated learning is also summarized, showing that overall, high-achieving students tend to set specific, process-oriented goals, self-monitor and self-evaluate during their learning, and seek help when needed. Finally, a model for training students to develop self-regulation is described.

References

Ames, R. (1983). Help-seeking and achievement orientation: Perspectives from attribution theory. In B. M. DePaulo, A. Nadler, & J. D. Fisher (Eds.), *New direction in helping. Volume 2: Help seeking* (pp. 165–186). New York: Academic Press.

Bandura, A. (1986). *Social foundations of thought and action: A social cognitive theory*. Englewood Cliffs, NJ: Prentice-Hall.

Boekaerts, M., Pintrich, P. R., & Zeidner, M. (2000). *Handbook of self-regulation*. San Diego, CA: Academic Press.

Cennamo, K. S., Ross, J. D., & Rogers, C. S. (2002). Evolution of a web-enhanced course: Incorporating strategies for self-regulation. *Educause Quarterly*, *25*(1), 28–33.

Ertmer, P. A. & Newby, T. J. (1996). The expert learner: Strategic, self-regulated, and reflective. *Instructional Science, 24*, 1–24.

Hattie, J., Biggs, J., & Purdie, N. (1996). Effects of learning skills interventions on student learning: A meta-analysis. *Review of Educational Research, 66,* 99–136.

Hofer, B. K., Yu, S. L., & Pintrich, P. R. (1998). Teaching college students to be self-regulated learners. In D. H. Schunk & B. J. Zimmerman (Eds.), *Self-regulated learning: From teaching to self-reflective practice* (pp. 57–85). New York: Guilford.

Karabenick, S. A., & Knapp, J. R. (1988). Effects of computer privacy on help seeking, *Journal of Applied Social Psychology, 18,* 461–472.

Kitsantas, A., & Chow, A. (2007). College students' perceived threat and preference for seeking help in traditional, distributed, and distance learning environments. *Computers and Education, 48*(3), 383–395.

Kitsantas, A., & Zimmerman, B. J. (1998). Self-regulation of motoric learning: A strategic cycle view. *Journal of Applied Sport Psychology, 10,* 220–239.

Kitsantas, A., Zimmerman, B. J., & Cleary, T. (2000). The role of observation and emulation in the development of athletic self-regulation. *Journal of Educational Psychology, 92*(4), 811–817.

Ley, K., & Young, D. B. (2001). Instructional principles for self-regulation. *Educational Technology, Research and Development, 49,* 93–103.

Loomis, K. D. (2000). Learning styles and asynchronous learning: Comparing the LASSI model to class performance. *Journal of Asynchronous Learning Networks, 4*(1), 23–32.

Pintrich, P. R. (2004). A conceptual framework for assessing motivation and self-regulated learning in college students. *Educational Psychology Review, 16,* 385–407.

Schunk, D. H., & Zimmerman, B. J. (Eds.) (1998). *Self-regulated learning: From teaching to reflective practice.* New York: Guilford Press.

Schunk, D. H., & Zimmerman, B. J. (Eds.) (2008). *Motivation and self-regulated learning: Theory, research, and applications.* Mahwah, NJ: Erlbaum.

Terry, K. P., & Doolittle, P. (2006). Fostering self-regulation in distributed learning. *College Quarterly, 9*(1). Retrieved January 3, 2008 from: http://www.collegequarterly.ca/2006-vol09-num01-winter/terry_doolittle.html

Whipp, J. L. & Chiarelli, S. (2004). Self-regulation in a web-based course: A case study. *Educational Technology Research and Development, 52*(4), 5–22.

Zimmerman, B. J. (2000). Attaining self-regulation: A social cognitive perspective. In M. Boekaerts, P. R. Pintrich, & M. Zeidner (Eds.), *Handbook of self-regulation* (pp. 13–39). San Diego, CA: Academic Press.

Zimmerman, B. J. (2008). Investigating self-regulation and motivation: Historical background, methodological developments, and future prospects. *American Educational Research Journal, 45*(1), 166–183.

Zimmerman, B. J., Bonner, S., & Kovach, R. (1996). *Developing self-regulated learners.* Washington, DC: American Psychological Association.

Zimmerman, B. J., Greenberg, D., & Weinstein, C. E. (1994). Self-regulating academic study time: A strategy approach. In D. H. Schunk & B. J. Zimmerman (Eds.), *Self-regulation of learning and performance: Issues and educational applications* (pp. 181–202). Hillsdale, NJ: Lawrence Erlbaum Associates.

Zimmerman, B. J., & Kitsantas, A. (1999). Acquiring writing revision skill: Shifting from process to outcome self-regulatory goals. *Journal of Educational Psychology, 91,* 1–10.

Zimmerman, B. J., & Schunk, D. H. (2008). Motivation: An essential dimension of self-regulated learning. In D. H. Schunk & B. J. Zimmerman (Eds.), *Motivation and self-regulated learning: Theory, research, and applications* (pp. 1–30). Mahwah, NJ: Erlbaum.

2

Defining Integrative Learning Technologies

Contents

Learning to Learn with Integrative Learning Technologies, pages 19–39
Copyright © 2010 by Information Age Publishing
All rights of reproduction in any form reserved.

19

Scenario

> *The digital revolution is far more significant than the invention of writing*
> *or even of printing. It offers the potential for humans to learn new ways*
> *of thinking and organizing social structures.*
>
> —Douglas Engelbart (1997)

Mark is a college professor in the English department. He teaches undergraduate introductory courses in English writing and composition. Mark's teaching approach has been primarily lecturing in a face-to-face context. He also models effective writing skills through selective reading assignments which students are required to discuss in class and provides extensive one-on-one feedback on his students' writing drafts during office hours. Recently however, his college adopted a Course Management System (CMS) and has asked that faculty use this CMS to support face-to-face course delivery so that students can have 24-hour access to course materials and activities. Many of Mark's students work full-time and hence would like to have unlimited access to the course content and assignments. Additionally, Mark is aware that his students are already using a variety of technologies to complete course-related activities and many have requested electronic feedback on their writing drafts.

Although Mark has used the CMS to post the course syllabus and assignment requirements, he feels that there is a lot more he can do to facilitate student learning using technology. The college has been offering workshops to bring faculty up to speed on the latest learning technologies. However, Mark feels overwhelmed because new technologies are continually emerging and his students seem to be much more technology-literate than he is. Mark is also concerned about the quality of his teaching. He believes that technology might not be able to effectively provide the personalized feedback that he typically gives his students in a face-to-face context. In addition, Mark realizes that in a technology-driven context he will not be able to directly observe student learning behaviors, which he relies on heavily to detect the type of help a student needs in order to achieve academically. So, how can Mark make the best use of learning technologies to meet his students' needs? More importantly, how can Mark use technology to prompt students to self-regulate their learning in order to improve their writing skills?

What Are Integrative Learning Technologies (ILT)?

Technological innovations are changing our learning spaces, interactions, and perspectives. Faculty and academic institutions can no longer depend on a single course or leaning management system (CMS or LMS) or curricular approach to deliver courses, support instructional events, and assess student learning. For example, today's students are demanding more engaging learning experiences and instantaneous access to information. Additionally, the traditional concept of the residential, full-time student is fading (The New Media Consortium & EDUCAUSE Learning Initiative, 2007). Johnson (2003b) posits that the one-size-fits-all industrial model of education is rapidly being replaced by a "service-economy model where learning is tailored to the learner" (p. 29). Furthermore, today's students experience or use technology very differently than do faculty. Hence, if faculty wish to gain students' attention, enable self-regulated learning, and sustain student motivation to learn, they must not only keep up with emerging technologies, but also learn how to use them creatively. This is a challenge that Mark and many other college instructors are facing.

So what are these technologies and how do they impact teaching and learning in online or blended learning environments? The term *Integrative Learning Technologies (ILT)* encompasses a multilayered and multipurpose approach to technology, yet is broad enough to include the more traditional learning technologies such as CMS or LMS, which have been ubiquitously adopted in higher-education contexts, as well as emerging learning technologies such as Web 2.0 and social media. Specifically, we define ILT as a dynamic collection or aggregation of Web tools, software applications, and mobile technologies that integrate technological and pedagogical features and affordances of the Internet and the World Wide Web to facilitate the design, development, delivery, and management of online and distributed learning.

In this context, distributed learning is defined as a course in which one or more of the instructional events that traditionally have occurred in the classroom are distributed such that learning may occur while students are separated by time or space from one another and/or the course instructor (Dede, 1996; Locatis & Weisberg, 1997). Distributed learning transcends the boundaries of traditional classroom settings so that learning can occur at the same time in different places (e.g., through scheduled video conferencing events), at different times in the same place (e.g., meeting face-to-face in the classroom to attend a series of guest lecturers or events), at different times in different places (e.g., using e-mail to communicate with the instructor and other students), or at the same time in the same place (e.g., meeting face-to-face in a physical classroom or in Second Life, a virtual world, for a regular class session) (Dabbagh & Bannan-Ritland, 2005). Simply stated, distributed learning is learning anytime, anywhere using various media.

ILT enables distributed learning by extending the benefits of an effective classroom environment beyond the physical campus setting and increasing the level of activity, engagement, and contact between instructors and students (Maslowski, Visscher, Collis, & Bloemen, 2000). Research shows that using ILT to support distributed learning events provides more opportunities for students to develop problem-solving and critical-thinking skills than do traditional classroom learning environments. Moreover, ILT has been found to positively influence student attendance, understanding, and interest in course content (Moore & Head, 2003). ILT also enables the integration of various types of content, resources, and learning experiences. For example, students can generate learning content using publishing tools such as weblogs (blogs) and wikis (social software tools), and can contribute, share, communicate, and collaborate through social networking utilities such as MySpace, Facebook, and LinkedIn. The emphasis of ILT is on active or collaborative media that support the shared creation of dynamic content and networked learning. Networked learning is similar to distributed learning. They both grew from the idea that human knowing is a social act resulting from individuals forming informal learning networks or communities of practice that support the decentralized or distributed concept of cognition (Shirky, 2003).

Overall, distributed or networked learning is improving access to learning opportunities, enhancing students' understanding and retention of new information, and targeting specific and rapidly changing educational needs (Johnson, 2003a). However, despite the perceived and documented benefits of distributed learning, some still think that distributed (and online) learning may diminish the quality of the educational experience. In this chapter, we argue that if instructional events are designed by harnessing the fundamentally communicative and information sharing attributes of ILT, distributed learning can provide new opportunities for learning interactions that were not perceived as possible in traditional teaching settings. For example, using ILT, instructors can (a) create opportunities for learners to interact with experts from around the world, (b) provide learners with instantaneous access to global resources, (c) allow learners the unprecedented opportunity to publish to a world audience, (d) take virtual field trips, (e) enable communication with a diverse audience, and (f) provide learners with the opportunity to share and compare information, negotiate meaning, and co-construct knowledge (Dabbagh & Bannan-Ritland, 2005). These learning opportunities can support and promote student use of the self-regulatory processes described in Chapter 1. We will demonstrate this more specifically in subsequent chapters of this book.

Faculty can design distributed learning environments using CMS or LMS such as Blackboard Learning Systems, Moodle, Sakai, ANGEL, Desire2Learn, and eCollege, which we consider to be a type or subset of ILT. These LMS, also known as an "enterprise technology" (Carmean & Brown, 2005), integrate several technological and pedagogical features that promote active and collaborative learning. Examples of such features include Web browsing, asynchronous and synchronous communication, personalized learning tools, experience and resource sharing tools, lesson and content generation tools, and administrative tools that allow tracking of student progress and course data. Additionally, LMS allow for different types of users (e.g., faculty, students, administrators, instructional designers) and for a multitude of Internet and web-based activities embedded within the system itself. Increasingly, LMS are integrating the newer Web 2.0 and social software tools (see Chapter 10) and more authentic assessment features (e.g., peer review, electronic portfolios, and grading rubrics), providing faculty with an even wider and more flexible array of tools to design online and distributed learning activities.

However, research has shown that college instructors who adopt an LMS to facilitate online and distributed learning are using very few of its features. Moreover, they are primarily using LMS features for information dissemination rather than in ways that engage students in meaningful and strategic or self-regulated learning (Apedoe, 2005; Boettcher, 2003; Dabbagh, 2005; Morgan, 2003; Oliver, 2001). Therefore, in order to (a) better understand the pedagogical potential of ILT and (b) consequently demonstrate to faculty and college instructors how to use ILT to design engaging instructional and learning activities that can enhance student self-regulatory skills, it is necessary to provide a pedagogically oriented classification of ILT. We describe this classification next.

A Pedagogical Classification of ILT

ILT can be classified into five broad pedagogical categories as follows (Dabbagh & Bannan-Ritland, 2005):

1. Collaborative and communication tools.
2. Content creation and delivery tools.
3. Administrative tools.
4. Learning tools.
5. Assessment tools.

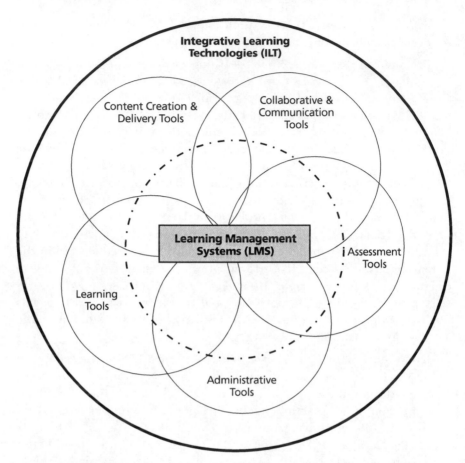

Figure 2.1 Relationship among ILT, LMS, and pedagogical tools categories.

Figure 2.1 depicts the relationship between ILT, LMS, and these five pedagogical categories. Specifically, Figure 2.1 shows that LMS (depicted by the dashed-line circle in the center) are a subset or special class of ILT, and that LMS integrate tools from the five broad and intersecting pedagogical categories. Figure 2.1 also illustrates that these categories extend beyond LMS to encompass emerging technologies and pedagogical practices at a broader level.

Collaborative and Communication Tools

This ILT category includes asynchronous and synchronous communication tools, social networking tools, and group tools. Asynchronous communication, from its simplest pedagogical standpoint, allows instructors and students at any time to post and review messages, respond to other messages, reflect or revise their responses, and modify their interpretations based on their reflections (Chamberlin, 2001). These pedagogical benefits or affordances are possible because of the time-delayed nature of asynchronous communication. Asynchronous communication is an inherent feature of Computer Mediated Communication (CMC) and has become an essential facility for distributed or networked learning. Asynchronous communication is enabled through technologies such as e-mail, threaded discussion forums, blogs (weblogs), wikis, and document- and calendar-sharing tools like Google Docs and Google Calendar, supporting one-to-one, one-to-many, and many-to-many interactions.

Synchronous communication, on the other hand, provides participants with the ability to interact in real time (as in face-to-face learning). Students and instructors sign on at the same time and are virtually present together in what is sometimes referred to as virtual or live sessions. Participants can discuss an issue, conduct presentations (using PowerPoint, for example), collaborate on a task or project, model or explain a procedure or concept, and engage in brainstorming or hypothesis-generating activities. Synchronous communication is more informal and spontaneous than asynchronous communication and is enabled through technologies such as chat, electronic whiteboards, instant messaging (IM), short message service (SMS), screen sharing, audio and video conferencing, and more recently, through virtual worlds such as Second Life. The Horizon report (The New Media Consortium & EDUCAUSE Learning Initiative, 2007) describes virtual worlds as the next wave in education experiences, providing a safe environment or "world" for students to explore, collaborate, role-play, and experience situations that are difficult or almost impossible to experience in a face-to-face classroom or in the physical world. Virtual worlds like Second Life and Croquet can also be considered spaces for distributed or networked learning that are more immersive than traditional collaborative and communication technologies.

Social networking tools (also known as social media) such as Facebook and MySpace have evolved into something more than social utilities that support communication with friends or network building. They cultivate what Wenger, McDermott, and Snyder (2002) describe as Communities of Practice (CoP) by enabling participants to find like-minded folks, exchange resources, build knowledge and identity, establish groups that support a common cause, and even change the course of national and international events if an organized effort (what Howard Rheingold refers to as Smart Mobs) materializes (Alexander, 2006; Shirky, 2003). Faculty need to become cognizant of the powerful and compelling impact of social networking tools and immersive virtual worlds and learn how to use them creatively to foster strategic learning and sustain student motivation in order to ensure academic success. If used purposefully and appropriately, social networking tools can be instrumental in increasing student access to and participation in course activities. These tools can promote truly engaging and meaningful learning activities by offering students opportunities to contribute knowledge, share ideas, and engage in collaborative problem solving and decision making. We discuss the types and characteristics of Web 2.0-enabled social networking tools in more detail in Chapter 10.

LMS such as Blackboard Learning System (e.g., CE 6.1 Enterprise) integrate several collaborative and communication tools including a discussion forum, a file exchange feature, real-time chat, internal e-mail, and a whiteboard. The discussion forum supports threaded discussions as well as blogging and journaling formats. Additionally, the discussion forum software has a spell checker, a HTML editor, and a text editor which enables formatting text as one would do in a word-processing application. The discussion forum software also supports the creation of mathematical equations and other scientific symbolisms (see www.edutools.info for more information on these LMS features and others).

Revisiting the scenario at the beginning of the chapter, Mark can use the discussion forum to engage his students in a formal discussion about a reading assignment that demonstrates good writing skills. He can ask students to comment on which sections of the reading they thought were well written and why. Mark can also use the file exchange feature to provide feedback on students' writing drafts and the whiteboard or chat features to provide more specific and personalized feedback on a student's writing draft in real time. Table 2.1 provides a list of examples of ILT collaborative and communication tools. Table 2.2 provides selected examples of how

TABLE 2.1   Examples of Collaborative and Communication Tools

Asynchronous tools	Synchronous tools	Group tools or social networking tools
• E-mail • Discussion forums • File exchange • Weblogs • Wikis • Document-sharing tools (e.g., Google Docs) • Calendar-sharing tools (e.g., Google Calendar)	• Real time chat or instant messaging tools (e.g., AIM) • Screen sharing tools (e.g., whiteboard) • SMS (short message service) • Virtual sessions (e.g., Adobe Connect)	• Community networking (e.g., MySpace, Facebook) • Group work tools or workspaces (e.g., Google Docs, wikis) • Immersive virtual worlds (e.g., Second Life and Active Worlds)

these tools can be used to support teaching and learning in online or distributed courses.

Content Creation and Delivery Tools

This ILT category includes tools for instructors that enable them to create, deliver, and manage web-based content and learning activities, and tools for students that enable them to contribute resources to the course website or resource-sharing area and submit assignments and journals. When used by students, content creation and delivery tools can serve as powerful learning strategies. They enable students to demonstrate their understanding of discipline-specific principles by developing content that synthesizes their knowledge, and designing complex individual and collaborative course projects that include interactive multimedia elements such as audio and video. For example, students can use HTML editors (e.g., Dreamweaver) as well as other Web publishing and media-sharing tools (e.g., weblogs, wikis, Flickr, YouTube, and Delicious) that facilitate the creation and sharing of learning content in a variety of formats such as podcasts and webcasts.

A concept related to the creation and sharing of content is that of a folksonomy. This concept is gaining prominence in the digital age due to the emergence of Web 2.0 content creation and delivery tools (or social media) such as Flickr, a photo-sharing tool, YouTube, a video-sharing tool, and Delicious, an online bookmark managing and sharing tool. Folksonomies are user-generated taxonomies and are dynamic and socially or collaboratively constructed, in contrast to established taxonomies that are typically created by experts in a discipline or domain of study. For example, the food pyramid is a well-established taxonomy created by the FDA (U.S. Food & Drug Administration). Even though the food pyramid has been revised several times, this is typically done by experts in the field of nutrition and is based on empirical research. Folksonomies, on the other hand, are subjective and relative classifications of things or artifacts (e.g., photos, documents, URLs) which emerge as a result of "personal free tagging" (Vander Wal, 2005) or "social tagging" (Seldow, 2007). Tagging is the ability for any user of a resource-sharing technology to label objects by entering a descriptor for that object in addition to its name. Other users can then label their objects using the same descriptors or search for objects using these descriptors, thereby creating a global collection of things that are linked or indexed by these tags or descriptors. This social tagging process or phenomenon has also been identified as sociosemantic networking (Seldow, 2007). Folksonomies therefore are a result of many users with different perspectives engaging in classifying a document or a digital object rather than relying on one individual (e.g., an expert or a cataloger) to set the

TABLE 2.2 Instructional Examples of Collaborative and Communication Tools

Tool or feature	Description	Instructional activity
Discussion forum Supports reflection, articulation, collaboration, social negotiation, and multiple perspectives	Allows students and instructors to discuss a topic by posting messages asynchronously to an online threaded discussion area • Messages are searchable and can be viewed by thread, topic, or date • File attachments are supported • Most have HTML and text editors and compile features allowing students and the instructor to download an entire discussion for further viewing and analysis • Some enable peer and instructor evaluation of postings, using a rating scale or a rubric	Instructors can use a discussion forum to facilitate a formal or structured online discussion linked to course content and can monitor and evaluate student participation Students can use a discussion forum to engage in an informal debate, share insights on a topic, and enrich their learning by experiencing new and multiple perspectives contributed by their classmates and the instructor
Virtual session (e.g., Macromedia Breeze), *chat* (e.g., AIM), or *whiteboard*	Allows students and instructors to communicate with each other in real time (synchronously) providing a more spontaneous method of interaction similar to face-to-face interactions	Instructors can use a whiteboard to visually explain or model a concept or process by displaying diagrams or charts for students who prefer graphic models over text-based explanations

Supports role-playing activities, problem solving, modeling and explaining, coaching, collaboration, and social negotiation	• Virtual session features include enabling instructors to set levels of participation from strictly one-way communication (e.g., broadcast, podcast, or webcast) to highly interactive sessions using screen sharing and breakout sessions where teams of students can discuss a problem raised in the virtual or chat session and rejoin the session to share their findings • Virtual session and some chat tools allow users to archive the session for future access and analysis	Instructors can use chat rooms to encourage student questions and provide immediate feedback, coaching, and clarification Instructors can assign students various roles to play (e.g., leader or moderator) or perspectives to take in mock debates that take place in a timed virtual session, breakout session, or chat session
Groupwork tools (e.g., document sharing tools such as Google Docs)	Allow instructors to organize a class into groups, provide group workspaces and presentation areas, and assign specific tasks or projects to different groups	Instructors can require students to use a document sharing tool to create a group document and engage in editing, adding content, and annotating the document (collaborative editing)
Support collaboration, teamwork, dynamic editing, problem solving, and scaffolding	• Random creation of student groups of a certain size or a set number of groups • Self-selection of students into a group • Associating a discussion forum, chat, or whiteboard area with a group • Allowing instructors to monitor groups	Students can upload draft documents in Google Docs, which accepts most popular file formats, and receive instructor and peer feedback

indexing terms for that object (Peterson, 2006). Hence folksonomies serve a different purpose than does a traditional taxonomy, functioning poorly in the creation of universal indices (such as library catalogs) yet brilliantly in connecting or linking concepts (Jones, 2007). Folksonomic classification using content creation and delivery tools can be a powerful teaching and learning strategy if an instructor's pedagogical approach is more constructivist (e.g., implementing a community of practice) than objectivist (e.g., primarily lecturing and testing).

LMS such as ANGEL integrate several content creation and delivery tools for both instructors and students. Examples include: course templates for setting up the course syllabus and content modules; a repository for content sharing, tagging, and reuse; instructional design tools for creating flexible learning sequences and designs; a student portfolio tool; and groupwork tools (see www.edutools.info for more information on these LMS features). Revisiting the scenario at the beginning of the chapter, Mark can use content creation and delivery tools to provide sample essays that demonstrate best practices in different writing genres (e.g., argumentation writing). He can also ask students to blog on a topic of interest to practice their writing skills. Mark can also ask his students to bookmark Web resources that illustrate best writing practices using Delicious and to tag these resources using a rating rubric. The class can then collectively generate a folksonomy of writing resources that is unique to the concepts and strategies learned in the course. Table 2.3 provides a list of examples of content creation and delivery tools. Table 2.4 provides selected examples of how these tools can be used to support teaching and learning in online or distributed courses.

Administrative Tools

This ILT category includes (a) tools to manage student information such as importing the class roster from the institution's registration system, updating or editing student info, assigning user IDs and passwords, tracking student navigation patterns and frequency of access to course materials and components, releasing grades, and generating an e-mail list; (b) tools to manage other users such as adding teaching assistants, graders, and course designers to the course and providing guest access; and (c) tools to manage course content and activities such as creating a course calendar, planning and releasing assignments, linking discussions to specific dates and course events, generating individual and group student work areas and discussion forums, personalizing access to specific course materials based on group membership, and managing the overall look and feel of the course.

TABLE 2.3   Examples of Content Creation and Delivery Tools

LMS tool types	Web publishing and resource sharing tools	Instructional design tools (embedded in most LMS)
• Course documents (uploading course documents) • Course information • Course announcements • Content module or learning unit creation and sequencing • Assignment dropbox or submission box • Presentation areas for students and groups to upload presentations and media creations • Course tasks and activities • Student portfolios or home pages	• HTML editors • Audio and video editors to generate podcasts and webcasts • Weblogs, wikis • Flickr (photosharing and tagging tool) • YouTube (video sharing and tagging tool) • Delicious (resource sharing and tagging tool) • Google Docs	• Tools that allow instructors to organize content into learning sequences such as the content module and learning units features • Tools that allow instructors to create reusable learning objects that can be shared through a central learning objects repository • Tools that allow instructors to reuse courses as templates for future lessons and courses • Tools that allow instructors to communicate learning goals and course objectives to students and connect those goals and objectives to assignments and assessment measures

LMS-specific administrative tools include an online calendar that both instructors and students can use to post events; an authentication feature that verifies user IDs and passwords; course authorization features that allow instructors and administrators to customize course access based on user roles; course-scheduling tools; and registration integration and student-tracking tools. Revisiting the scenario at the beginning of the chapter, Mark can use the online calendar to plan the writing assignments and activities for his students. He can also use the course scheduler tool in conjunction with the online calendar tool to break down the writing assignments, related resources, and evaluation criteria weekly and monthly to help students successfully reach the goal of completing the final course essay. Additionally, if Mark is designing a collaborative writing assignment, he can suggest

TABLE 2.4 Instructional Examples of Content Creation and Delivery Tools

Tool or feature	Description	Instructional activity
Weblogs or blogs Support articulation and reflection	Provide students with a structured web-based medium for creative expression and journaling • Blogs are a web-based personal journaling or publishing system that allows users to express their opinions about a variety of issues • Blogs are typically archived chronologically and can be open for others to comment on	Engage students in writing, reflection, and articulation, by requiring students to blog about the course readings as a form of journaling
Wikis (e.g., Wikipedia) Support articulation, reflection, collaboration, and content generation	Provide students and instructors with a web-based, collaborative editing environment • Wikis are a collection of Web pages that are modifiable or editable • Students can create, edit, and manage content • Privileges can be set to determine who has editing access	Engage students in a collaborative activity to prepare a research proposal by setting up a wiki to support the creation, editing, and management of the proposal Student teams can provide the URL of a project wiki to an expert of their choice (or an instructor-recommended expert) and give editing privileges to the expert to solicit additional feedback on project work
Content module or learning units (LMS content creation features)	Enables instructors to organize course materials into structurally meaningful units, such as objectives, syllabus, prior work examples, learning materials, and assignments	Students can locate materials such as prior work examples that provide models of "best practices" Sequence instructional materials and learning activities so that students can proceed through the content in a self-paced manner
Course syllabus (LMS feature)	Enables instructors to use a template to define course goals, objectives, and activities	Students and instructors use the syllabus to organize and schedule learning activities

---

TABLE 2.5   Examples of Administrative Tools

- *Calendar tools* (e.g., course calendar and Google Calendar) that allow instructors to provide a timeline of events, activities, and required outputs to help students manage their time and learning tasks
- *Course planning and scheduling tools* that allow instructors to provide a bird's-eye view of the course components and events and use labels and names for content areas that make the course components and resources more meaningful, relevant, and easier to locate
- *Discussion management tools* that allow instructors to set up moderated discussions in a course, assign specific students to a discussion, and set the beginning and end dates of a discussion
- *Authentication and authorization tools* that provide instructors with the capability to allow guest access to a course, and assign user roles such as teaching assistants, graders, or instructional designers, by controlling or customizing their level of access in an LMS
- *Course management tools* that allow instructors to do the following:
    a. Selectively release assignments, assessments, and announcements based on specific start and stop dates and on preselected criteria (e.g., date and grade)
    b. Link discussions to specific dates or course events
    c. Personalize access to specific course materials based on group membership, previous course activity, or student performance
    d. Customize the look and feel of the course by using embedded templates to tailor the color schemes, navigation icons, menu items, etc.
- *Student tracking tools* that allow instructors to track the frequency and duration of student access to individual course components and gather usage statistics that can be aggregated across the entire course as well as across other courses
- *Student enrollment and registration tools* that allow instructors to pull a class roster from the university's registration system and/or allow students to self-enroll or audit a course

---

that students use Google Docs and Google Calendar to organize their tasks and timelines. Table 2.5 provides examples of administrative tools and how instructors can use them in an instructional or course context.

Learning Tools

This ILT category includes tools primarily for learners to create personalized learning experiences or PLEs. In the process of exploring course content, working on assignments, and participating in learning activities, students can use a variety of learning tools, and apply a variety of task strategies to process and organize the content in a meaningful way. Learning tools can be thought of as tools that enable learners to manipulate content online in contrast to tools that allow students to post end-products such as assignments and tests. The ability to annotate text while exploring course content, take notes (online), bookmark and link information, perform a contextualized search, and build a personal folder of relevant course material are examples of learning tools.

Learning tools can be classified into three types: content collection or aggregation tools, exploratory tools, and personalized tools. Content collection or aggregation tools include tools that enable individual compilation or aggregation of course materials and resources. For example, the social bookmarking tool Delicious allows students to save bookmarks to a public website and tag the bookmarks with keywords to organize them meaningfully. Students can link to other students' bookmarks that have been tagged with a similar keyword. Online journaling is another example of content collection and aggregation tools. Students can create journals in the form of weblogs or wikis to develop an archive of commentary regarding a particular learning issue or topic. Google Calendar can also be considered an example of a content collection and aggregation tool. Students can use Google Calendar to aggregate their schedules and project tasks when working in groups. LMS-specific content collection or aggregation tools include the online discussion "compile and download" feature and a "work offline" feature that allows students to download the content for an entire course into a format that can be printed or stored locally.

Exploratory learning tools include tools that enable contextualized (course-specific) search tools, help tools, and resource sharing tools such as social networking tools. For example, students can use social networking tools such as Facebook to set up special interest groups and networks in order to support informal learning and resource sharing. LMS-specific exploratory learning tools include a search tool that allows students to search course content and discussion threads, and help tools that provide context-sensitive help for any course tool. Personalized learning tools include tools that allow the creation of a personalized course glossary or indexing scheme (e.g., a site map); RSS (Rich Site Summary) feed readers that can be customized to receive preselected information; note-taking and annotation tools; and a portfolio tool that allows students to selectively display their course work.

Revisiting the scenario at the beginning of this chapter, Mark can encourage his students to use learning tools in a variety of ways. For example, he can provide students with the ability to annotate each others' writing drafts using the note-taking tool to promote peer feedback. Mark can also help his students create a personal folder to provide a central location or

TABLE 2.6   Examples of Learning Tools

Content collection or aggregation tools	Exploratory learning tools	Personalized tools
• Bookmarking tools (e.g., Delicious) • Compile and download tools • Google Calendar	• Search tools • Help tools • Resource tools • Community networking tools	• RSS feeds • Student portfolios • Note-taking tools • Glossary tools • Indexing tools • Personal calendar

repository for their writing drafts and notes. Tables 2.6 and 2.7 provide examples of learning tools and how instructors can use them in online and distributed courses.

Assessment Tools

This ILT category includes a variety of assessment tools ranging from supporting the creation of traditional tests to the development of more authentic performance-based assessments such as e-portfolios. LMS-specific assessment tools include test-type tools that support multiple choice, matching, fill-in-the-blank, and short-answer questions as well as essay tests. In addition, LMS features support the development of test questions that include media such as images, video, and audio. Instructors can also customize question types, randomize questions and answers, set a time limit on a test, permit multiple attempts, allow students to review past attempts at a quiz, and specify whether correct responses are displayed as feedback.

Examples of LMS-authentic assessment tools include the capability to create self-assessments, peer-assessments, and performance-based assessments using a variety of rubric scales and customized grading schemes. Self-assessments can be in the form of reflection journals and e-portfolios or weblogs. Instructors can also generate surveys to assess individual contributions to group work and collect student feedback on the course for formative evaluation purposes. LMS also include assessment tools that allow instructors to report grades per assignment and class averages and totals per assignment or test as well as percentages of the overall course grade. Instructors can download grading areas as a single file and import the file into a database or spreadsheet program for further analyses. Students can also use these grade-reporting LMS features to track their performance by checking grades periodically.

TABLE 2.7 Instructional Examples of Learning Tools

Tool or feature	Description	Instructional activity
Online notes or journal within a course (an LMS feature)	Enables students to attach notes to any page in the course website (similar to PowerPoint notes) or make notes in a personal online journal • Students can choose to share personal journal entries with their instructor or other students or keep their entries private • Students can combine their notes with the course content to create a printable study guide	Students can create their own annotations on course materials or keep a learning journal in order to reinforce their learning and understanding of course material
Bookmarks within a course (an LMS feature)	Enables students to create personalized bookmarks within or outside a course (i.e., on the Web) to facilitate ease of access to important study materials • Students can choose to share their bookmarks with the instructor or other students	Students can assemble a list of links (bookmarks) that reference study materials within the course content and on the Web in preparation for an assignment or a test
Collect or compile feature	Allows students to combine selected messages from the discussion board into a single text file	Students can use the resulting "collected" file to search for key words and juxtapose congruent or opposing ideas within the texts
Personal calendar or Personal tasks feature	Allows students to develop a personal schedule of learning activities	Students can increase their autonomy and self-directed learning capacity by setting their own work/study timetables in support of learning outcomes
Community or social networking tools (e.g., Facebook, MySpace)	Allows students to create networks that are tailored to their interests and learning needs. These networks can then become informal learning environments and support systems for building resources and collaborating	Students can create online clubs and interest and study groups at the system level to interact in system-wide chat rooms or discussion forums

TABLE 2.8   Examples of Assessment Tools

Traditional assessment tools	Authentic assessment tools
Test-generation tools that support multiple-choice test formats as well as short-answer, fill-in-the-blank, matching, and essay questions	*Portfolio tools*—Students can use weblogs to reflect on their learning and Web 2.0 tools such as podcasting to record their learning activities
Survey design tools that support customized questions and allow instructors to collect evaluative information about their course	*Progress tools*—Students can review their progress by checking their grades and the instructor feedback periodically and reflect on their learning strategies and outcomes
Online marking tools that allow instructors a variety of options for marking tests and quizzes, including the options of anonymously evaluating student responses and allowing students to rate and comment on other student submissions	*Monitoring tools*—Students can use these tools to determine the amount of time spent in each component of the course and to identify whether they have missed any reading sections or have spent sufficient time on materials
Online gradebook that allows instructors to customize grading for each assignment or test, perform statistical analysis on grades, and export scores to an external spreadsheet	*Self assessment tools*—Students can use these tools to test their knowledge in order to identify areas of conceptual weakness and instructors can use these tools to provide students with evaluative feedback without formally assessing results

Revisiting the scenario at the beginning of the chapter, Mark can use authentic assessment tools by providing students with individual portfolio spaces to which students can upload their writing drafts and receive instructor and peer feedback. Mark can also use this portfolio area to monitor student progress by comparing new drafts to older drafts to see whether students have integrated his feedback and/or peer feedback. To facilitate this feedback process, Mark can develop a customized rubric using the survey tool that explicitly states the criteria for the writing assignment and associates the criteria with a Likert-type scale. This scale can then be used by students as a self-assessment tool to monitor their progress, by peers to provide feedback on each other's drafts, and by Mark to provide instructor feedback. Table 2.8 provides examples of assessment tools and their instructional uses in online and distributed courses.

Conclusion

This chapter provided an overview of ILT. It also addressed the role of ILT in supporting and facilitating learning in online or distributed courses. A pedagogically oriented classification of ILT consisting of five key categories is presented and each category is described in detail. Additionally, specific examples of how instructors can use ILT tools and features within each ILT category to develop technology-mediated learning tasks and activities are provided.

References

Alexander, B. (2006). Web 2.0: A new wave of innovation for teaching and learning? EDUCAUSE Review, *41*(2), 32–44. Retrieved June 13, 2006, from: http://www.educause.edu/ir/library/pdf/ERM0621.pdf

Apedoe, X. S. (2005). The interplay of teaching conceptions and course management system design: Research implications and creative innovations for future designs. In P. McGee, C. Carmean, & A. Jafari (Eds.), *Course management systems for learning: Beyond accidental pedagogy* (pp. 57–68). Hershey, PA: Idea Group, Inc.

Boettcher, J. V. (2003, July). Course management systems and learning principles: Getting to know each other. *Syllabus, 33–36.*

Carmean, C., & Brown, G. (2005). Measure for measure: Assessing course management systems. In P. McGee, C. Carmean, & A. Jafari (Eds.), *Course management systems for learning: Beyond accidental pedagogy* (pp. 1–13). Hershey, PA: Idea Group, Inc.

Chamberlin, W. S. (2001). Face-to-face vs. cyberspace: Finding the middle ground. *Syllabus, 15*(5), 10–11 & 32.

Dabbagh, N. (2005). Pushing the envelope: Designing authentic learning activities using Course Management Systems. In P. McGee, C. Carmean, & A. Jafari (Eds.), *Course management systems for learning: Beyond accidental pedagogy* (pp. 171–189). Hershey, PA: Idea Group, Inc.

Dabbagh, N., & Bannan-Ritland, B. (2005). *Online learning: Concepts, strategies, and application.* Upper Saddle River, NJ: Prentice-Hall.

Dede, C. (1996). Emerging technologies and distributed learning. *American Journal of Distance Education, (10)*2, 4–36.

Johnson, D. F. (2003a). Toward a philosophy of online education. In D. G. Brown (Ed.), *Developing faculty to use technology: Programs and strategies to enhance teaching* (pp. 9–11). Hoboken, NJ: Wiley.

Johnson, D. F. (2003b). The ethics of teaching in an online environment. In D. G. Brown (Ed.), *Developing faculty to use technology: Programs and strategies to enhance teaching* (pp. 27–31). Hoboken, NJ: Wiley.

Jones, A. (2007). *The new metadata: Folksonomic classification of learning objects.* Unpublished manuscript, George Mason University, Fairfax, VA.

Locatis, C., & Weisberg, M. (1997). Distributed learning and the Internet. *Contemporary Education, 68*(2), 100–103.

Maslowski, R., Visscher, A. J., Collis, B., & Bloemen, P. M. (2000). The formative evaluation of a web-based course-management system within a university setting. *Educational Technology, 40*(3), 5–19.

Moore, A. H., & Head, J. T. (2003). Philosophy of faculty development at Virginia Tech. In D. G. Brown (Ed.), *Developing faculty to use technology: Programs and strategies to enhance teaching* (pp. 4–5). Hoboken, NJ: Wiley.

Morgan, G. (2003). *Faculty use of course management systems.* Boulder, CO: ECAR Research Publication.

New Media Consortium & EDUCAUSE Learning Initiative (2007). *The 2007 Horizon report.* Retrieved December 14, 2007 from: http://www.nmc.org/pdf/2007_Horizon_Report.pdf

Oliver, K. (2001). Recommendations for student tools in online course management systems. *Journal of Computing in Higher Education, 13*(1), 47–70.

Peterson, E. (2006). Beneath the Metadata: Some philosophical problems with folksonomy. *D-Lib Magazine, 12*(11). Retrieved June 21, 2008 from: http://www.dlib.org/dlib/november06/peterson/11peterson.html

Seldow, A. (2007). *Social tagging in education and the workplace.* Paper presented at the 3rd annual e-Learning Symposium. George Mason University, Fairfax, VA.

Shirky, C. (2003, October). *Work on networks: A GBN tour by Clay Shirky.* A GBN (Global Business Network) Report. Retrieved January 23, 2008 from: http://www.gbn.com/GBNDocumentDisplayServlet.srv?aid=13227&url=%2FUploadDocumentDisplayServlet.srv%3Fid%3D13976

Vander Wal, T. (2005). *Folksonomy definition and Wikipedia.* Retrieved June 19, 2008 from: http://www.vanderwal.net/random/entrysel.php?blog=1750

Wenger, E., McDermott, R., & Snyder, W. (2002). *Cultivating communities of practice: A guide to managing knowledge.* Cambridge, MA: Harvard Business School Press.

3

Self-Regulatory Training with Integrative Learning Technologies
A Theory-Based Model

Contents

Learning to Learn with Integrative Learning Technologies, pages 41–55
Copyright © 2010 by Information Age Publishing
All rights of reproduction in any form reserved.

Scenario

> *I never teach my pupils; I only attempt to provide the conditions*
> *in which they can learn.*
> —Albert Einstein

Sylvia, a college professor, has been using Integrative Learning Technologies (ILT) for over ten years. During the fourth semester week of teaching a remedial algebra course, she realized that although the majority of her students were technologically proficient, about 80 percent were not utilizing ILT to successfully complete the course requirements. For example, like many instructors who are comfortable with ILT, Sylvia had incorporated unique tools into her course design that students could use to scaffold their learning. However, even with anytime, anywhere access to these tools, Sylvia's students were submitting late, incomplete, inaccurate assignments, and they were not asking questions or accessing relevant resources in a timely manner. In other words, they were not consciously or systematically using ILT to learn how to learn. Sylvia began to question whether she was effectively using ILT to promote self-regulated learning in her students.

Upon reflection, Sylvia decided to create opportunities through the use of ILT by redesigning several assignments to incorporate self-regulated learning processes. For example, in an assignment focusing on function domains, Sylvia used ILT to prompt students to set process goals and to model strategies that students could use to master related concepts. In addition, Sylvia used ILT to provide detailed feedback on student progress toward achieving their goals. Sylvia's new approach helped her students become responsible learners by enabling them to systematically select effective task strategies and to self-monitor, self-evaluate, and modify their learning efforts accordingly. Consequently, Sylvia's students became better equipped to use these learned skills to succeed in future courses and beyond in their professional careers.

Academic Self-Regulation and ILT

In Chapter 1 we described self-regulated learning, provided an array of self-regulatory processes, and described how these processes are embedded within a three-phase conceptual model and a four-phase training model of self-regulation. In Chapter 2, we defined ILT, presented a pedagogical classification of ILT, and provided examples of how ILT tools and components can be used to design engaging and meaningful instructional activities. This chapter integrates empirical research on self-regulation and ILT to provide a unique perspective on how these two areas connect to bridge the gap between theory and practice. This chapter also demonstrates how instructors can use the pedagogical categories of ILT to train students to become self-regulated learners in online, blended, or distributed learning environments in order to promote academic success.

Statistics show that 83 percent of undergraduates surveyed in 2006 ($n = 27,846$) used a CMS or LMS such as WebCT, ANGEL, or Blackboard several times a week (Salaway, Borreson-Caruso, & Nelson, 2007). Moreover, 81.6 percent of the undergraduates surveyed used a social utility (e.g., Facebook or MySpace) daily. Given these statistics, it is imperative to teach students to engage in self-regulated learning in order to promote academic success in these increasingly technology-driven learning environments. In traditional face-to-face contexts, faculty can gather information about their students' study skills through personal interactions and observations and can teach students self-regulation skills through a variety of instructional methods (Dabbagh & Kitsantas, 2004). However, in distributed, blended, or online learning environments, it becomes more difficult for faculty to assess students' learning behaviors and for students to discern the instructor's expectations. Additionally, the physical absence of the instructor places increased demands on students to achieve learning tasks independently, particularly for students with low self-regulatory skills (Kauffman, 2002). Hence, instructors must stay apprised of the pedagogical potential of ILT and leverage them to develop self-regulated students to ensure academic success. Furthermore, instructors must keep up with the technological focus of today's students, referred to as the millennial generation or digital natives (Prensky, 2001).

Research on Self-Regulated Learning and ILT

Research evidence shows that technology-enriched learning designed to enhance student self-regulation and motivation facilitates academic performance and increases positive attitudes toward learning (Henry, 1995; Kramarski & Gutman, 2006; López-Morteo & López, 2007). However in a "just-in-time, needs-driven world, students need a broad base of understanding, a demonstrated ability to learn a wide variety of subjects, and a proven track record of learning how to learn" (Johnson, 2003a, p. 11). While online education presents important opportunities to teach a mobile population, it must be designed on clearly conceived concepts. In addition, online education should consider how to replicate what is most valued in face-to-face instruction particularly those interactions that help students become successful and independent learners.

When an instructor integrates online and distributed learning interactions in a course, students must figure out how to complete assignments without the visual cues and body language of the instructor. Additionally, students must also learn how to function independently, self-initiate their own learning, communicate effectively without the cues of proximity, and learn how to use the necessary technologies and strategies to succeed in the course (Johnson, 2003b). In essence, students must learn how to learn or self-regulate. Therefore, instructors must actively develop strategies and practices to support strategic learning using technology. Specifically, instructors should design course assignments and learning activities such that they are tailored to the task complexity (Choi, Land, & Turgeon, 2005), and include the capability to diagnose, guide, and evaluate different processes of self-regulation as well as be able to activate student prior knowledge and use of metacognitive learning strategies (Azevedo, et al., 2005). Referring back to the scenario at the beginning of this chapter, Sylvia realized that her students did not know how to self-regulate their learning; she therefore used ILT to design assignments that facilitated the development of student self-regulatory skills. Additionally, in online or distributed learning, instructional habits that we as faculty and instructors take for granted in traditional face-to-face courses become critical instructional events that require careful design and implementation. For example, the steps we typically take to facilitate student interactions with the learning content, such as developing course assignments, providing students with feedback, communicating learning expectations, and promoting social interaction, require a different pedagogical approach when using ILT (Johnson, 2003b).

Although research surrounding self-regulated learning and use of ILT is at its initial stages (Azevedo, 2005), this research shows the powerful potential that ILT have as teaching tools for instructors and learning tools for students. Azevedo (2005) describes computerized environments that attempt to engage students in higher-order cognitive processes, goal setting, and effective task strategies as metacognitive tools. A review of the literature shows that computerized environments that use ILT as metacognitive tools not only contribute to student achievement, but when designed properly can also help students develop specific study skills and self-regulated learning processes such as goal setting, self-monitoring, and self-evaluation (Chang, 2007; Dabbagh & Kitsantas, 2005; Kitsantas & Dabbagh, 2004; Perry & Winne, 2006; Winne, 2006; Winne et al., 2006). For example, Chang (2007) argues that online learning must be designed to facilitate student self-regulatory processes in order to promote achievement and retention. Specifically, Chang examined how self-monitoring influenced web-based language learning with 99 Taiwanese college students enrolled in an English class. The results revealed that regardless of the level of English proficiency, students who had used self-monitoring strategies achieved at a higher level than students who did not use self-monitoring strategies. Furthermore, students who had lower levels of English proficiency had benefitted more from using self-monitoring strategies than students with higher proficiency levels. This suggests that including self-regulatory processes into the design of online learning significantly improves academic outcomes.

Research also shows that different categories of ILT support different self-regulation processes (Dabbagh & Kitsantas, 2005; Kitsantas & Dabbagh, 2004). Specifically, Kitsantas and Dabbagh (2004) and Dabbagh and Kitsantas (2005) conducted two studies involving 80 and 65 college students respectively. These students were enrolled in a total of eight LMS-supported undergraduate and graduate courses. In both studies, students were asked to indicate which self-regulatory processes (e.g., goal setting, self-monitoring, time management) were supported or promoted through the use of LMS features based on the ILT categories described in Chapter 2 (i.e., collaborative and communication tools, content creation and delivery tools, administrative tools, assessment tools, and learning tools).

The results of the first study (Kitsantas & Dabbagh, 2004) revealed that (a) administrative tools (e.g., course planning and scheduling tools such as the online calendar) supported the use of self-monitoring and help seeking; (b) collaborative and communication tools (e.g., e-mail, discussion forums, and document sharing and file exchange tools) were more useful in supporting goal setting, help seeking, and time management; (c) content creation and delivery tools (i.e., instructional design tools and resource sharing and Web publishing tools) were reported as particularly helpful for self-evaluation, task strategies, and goal setting; and (d) learning tools (e.g., bookmarking tools, search tools, and help tools) were reported as more useful in supporting task strategies. Furthermore, the results of the second study revealed that assessment tools (e.g., student portfolios and online gradebook) supported task strategies, self-monitoring, and self-evaluation. Table 3.1 summarizes the results of this research.

TABLE 3.1   ILT-Supported Self-Regulatory Processes

ILT category	Self-regulatory process
Administrative tools	Self-monitoring, help seeking
Collaborative and communication tools	Goal setting, help seeking, time management
Content creation and delivery tools	Self-evaluation, task strategies, goal setting
Learning tools	Task strategies
Assessment tools	Task strategies, self-monitoring, self-evaluation

Additionally, in the Dabbagh and Kitsantas (2005) study, qualitative results complemented the quantitative results revealing the usefulness of ILT features in supporting self-regulation while completing specific course assignments. For example, students perceived content creation and delivery tools useful in scaffolding the self-regulated learning processes of help seeking, task strategies, self-evaluation, and goal setting, while completing assignments involving problem-solving tasks. Students also perceived collaborative and communication tools useful in supporting help seeking and time management, while completing collaborative or team-based assignments.

The results of these studies have significant implications on using ILT features to support or promote student self-regulation. Knowing which self-regulatory processes are supported using ILT categories can assist instructors in providing the scaffolding needed to promote student self-regulation in online and distributed learning contexts as well as target and improve specific self-regulatory processes. As Brooks (1997) argues, "You can't place your materials on the Web if your candidate students are not self-regulating and hope for success" (p. 135). Therefore, self-regulated learning can greatly impact students' successful engagement in the types of learning tasks required in online and distributed learning contexts (Hartley & Bendixen, 2001). After all, studies (e.g., Whipp & Chiarelli, 2004) show that students use and adapt traditional self-regulated learning processes to complete learning tasks in online courses. Therefore, it is important to understand how specific technology features can enhance specific self-regulatory processes. Table 3.2 provides general examples of how ILT can be used to support student self-regulation.

The research reviewed in this section clearly supports the need to develop instructional interventions that align with the pedagogical categories of ILT to promote or foster self-regulated learning and motivation, particularly in college freshman remedial mathematics courses where students

TABLE 3.2 Mapping Self-Regulatory Processes to ILT

Self-regulation processes	Associated ILT category	Examples of instructors' role in supporting self-regulation	Examples of students' use of ILT
Goal setting	Collaborative and communication tools	• Help students identify and set learning goals	• Students use e-mail to communicate goals to instructor and receive feedback
Task strategies	Learning tools	• Help students select appropriate strategies	• Students use a social bookmarking tool (e.g., Delicious) to organize learning resources
	Content creation and delivery tools	• Help students interact meaningfully with content material	• Students use graphics, audio, and video to view and process learning content (e.g., downloading or creating a podcast or webcast)
Self-monitoring	Learning tools	• Help students monitor progress	• Students use the LMS-compile feature to archive a discussion forum and reread it to monitor comprehension
	Assessment tools		• Students check their grades online to monitor progress
Self-evaluating	Assessment tools	• Help students evaluate their work	• Students use self assessment tools to evaluate their learning
	Content creation and delivery tools		• Students use e-portfolios to reflect on their learning and receive feedback from instructors and peers

need the most support to succeed. Previous technology-enhanced interventions were limited in their capability for supporting on demand or anytime, anywhere access and/or subject- or assignment-specific feedback and guidance. More important, they did not specifically address the development of students' self-regulatory skills and motivation in postsecondary remedial mathematics courses, which is the challenge that Sylvia is facing.

Training Students to Become Self-Regulated Learners with ILT

Academic skills such as writing a research paper or learning how to solve a math problem is acquired initially by watching a skilled instructor perform the task and by listening to the instructor explain how to accomplish the task. In other words, through modeling, learners have the opportunity to observe a demonstration of the desired behavior as performed by an expert (Bandura, 1997). Below, we describe how Sylvia can use ILT to help her students develop self-regulation skills and subsequently achieve academic success through the four-phase self-regulation training model briefly described in Chapter 1. Sylvia's is a remedial class; students have been placed there because they have had difficulty learning algebra concepts and are not motivated to stay on task. In addition, the class is too large to allow for personalized instructor support. Consequently, Sylvia's opportunities for helping students develop effective study skills are greatly diminished.

The self-regulation training model has been specifically designed to support the metacognitive, motivational and behavioral aspects of learning (Zimmerman, 2000). Having systematic support in these areas is highly needed in postsecondary remedial courses such as Sylvia's. The model consists of the following four phases: (1) observation, (2) emulation, (3) self-control, and (4) self-regulation. Figure 3.1 illustrates the phases of this model and the role of the instructor, the student, and ILT in each phase.

In order for instructors to effectively train students using ILT according to the four-phase model, they must first prepare. That is, instructors must review the material that students need to learn and think about the best approach to present and teach the information. In designing the course and choosing the instructional strategies, an instructor must extensively review the nature of the domain, context, and task. In other words, the instructional approach must be based on domain-, context-, and task-specific considerations. This is because the strategies and learning activities required for effective and efficient instruction can differ across domains and tasks. Figure 3.1 describes a preparation phase in which instructors begin by per-

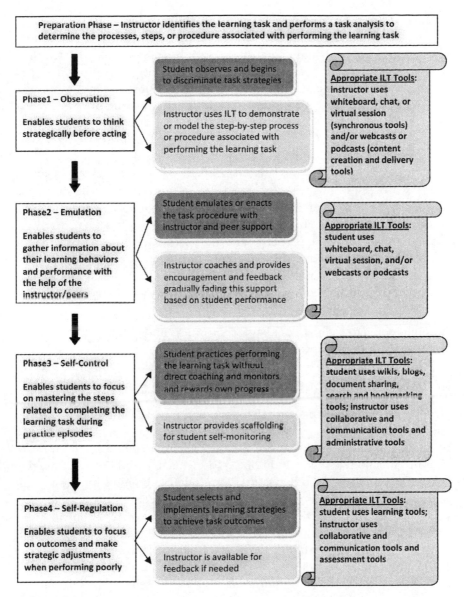

Figure 3.1 A model of self-regulated learning illustrating the role of the instructor, the student, and ILT.

forming a task analysis to identify the processes or steps associated with the learning task that they want students to accomplish.

During the observation phase, or phase 1 of the model, the instructor uses appropriate ILT categories and components to model the task processes, thereby allowing students to vicariously experience the steps or procedure needed to complete the task. In phase 2 of the training model, emulation, students begin enacting the task processes using ILT features, becoming aware of the self-regulatory processes of goal setting and task strategies. In this phase, students interact with the instructor and peers to seek help and clarification as needed. Additionally, instructors observe student performance using ILT and provide coaching and feedback to ensure appropriate enactment of task processes. In phase 3 of the training model, self-control, students spend most of their time using ILT to practice the expert- or instructor-modeled behaviors on their own and focus on mastering the task processes. It may be necessary during this phase for the instructor to provide a checklist or criteria to ensure that students can accurately assess their performance. During self-regulation, the last phase of the training model, students become proactive and independent learners who are able to focus primarily on outcomes and adjust their strategy as needed. They accomplish this by using appropriate ILT tools and components in a cyclical and proactive way, self-reflecting in response to unsatisfactory outcomes.

Next we describe how Sylvia uses ILT to implement the four-phase training model to facilitate her students' understanding of a difficult mathematics concept such as function domains.

An Illustration of Self-Regulatory Training Using ILT

One of the most misunderstood topics in remedial college mathematics courses is function domains. For example, when studying this topic, students often do not understand that the question being asked is: For what set of x's is this function defined? Additionally, students have difficulty transferring ideas about functions to other settings and other families of functions. This makes it difficult for students to fully grasp the concept of the domain of x, which is an important aspect of understanding functions. According to Ayers, Davis, Dubinsky, and Lewin (1988), understanding the concept of functions requires students to be able to think of a function as both a process and a single entity or mental object. The concept of functions must be consciously understood, which is why the four-phase model of self-regulation is an appropriate instructional or training model in this case. So how can Sylvia apply this model using ILT to help her students understand this concept?

In preparation, Sylvia selects a real-world problem to facilitate students' understanding of the application of function domains. This approach is designed to stimulate student interest and motivation to learn a seemingly irrelevant concept. Sylvia frames the material in this way: "The function below represents cellular phone subscriptions from 1990 to 2001: $y = 6.4194$

$(1.3395)^x$. For what set of x values does this function work?" This question requires students to determine the domain of a function, but it is framed or contextualized in a real-world context that students can relate to. Additionally, Sylvia performs a task analysis to determine the strategic steps involved in understanding function domains. She identifies the following steps: (1) identify patterns, (2) create a table, and (3) depict a graph to model the function. Now Sylvia is ready to implement the model using ILT.

In the observation phase, Sylvia models or demonstrates the three steps involved in the learning task using ILT. She videotapes herself (using a webcam) demonstrating the three steps, uploads the video to YouTube, and provides a link to the students so they can view the video as many times as they wish. In her demonstration, she uses a standard classroom blackboard and verbalizes the process as she would normally in a face-to-face classroom session. She rewrites the function as $F(x) = 6.4194 \ (1.3395)^x$ to emphasize that x is the domain of a function, that is, the set of all possible input values which in this case is the set of years {1990, 1991, 1992, 1993, 1994, 1995, 1996, 1997, 1998, 1999, 2000, 2001}; and $F(x)$ is the output range or the set of cellular phone subscriptions in those years since each year gives a unique number of cellular phone subscriptions. Sylvia plugs in a few values for x that lie within the range of years 1990–2001 and uses the scientific calculator to calculate the output (y value or $F(x)$). She models how this step provides information about the pattern of the function (e.g., whether the output is increasing or decreasing, and by how much).

Next, Sylvia begins to create a table with these values (the second step). In the first row of the table she lists the domain values (the years) and in the second row she lists the number of cellular phone subscriptions that she calculated for the values in the first step. Then she continues to calculate the output values for the remaining years until she has an output value for each input value. Finally, she uses graphing paper to plot the function using the values from the table to determine the range, the third step. A less sophisticated content creation and delivery tool, if instructors do not have access to a webcam or a camcorder, is a narrated PowerPoint (PPT) presentation developed using an LMS course documents or content module feature or a Word or PDF document that explains the three steps involved in understanding function domains.

Alternatively, instructors can use collaborative and communication tools, specifically the screen-sharing whiteboard tool or a virtual session tool such as Wimba or Adobe Connect to model similar steps. This would give students the opportunity to ask questions as they are observing the modeling process. However, given the large number of students in Sylvia's class, she may want to schedule multiple virtual sessions as well as provide this demonstration asynchronously, via YouTube or a similar video sharing tool as suggested earlier. This allows students to watch the demonstration at their own pace as well as replay segments.

For the emulation phase of the four-phase training model, Sylvia decides to place students in small groups and schedule virtual sessions with each group so that students can enact the task processes of the cell phone function domain example while she observes and monitors their performance. Students can designate a group leader to enact the steps or divide the steps among themselves. Using a synchronous tool enables the instructor to provide immediate coaching and the students to ask questions, both of which are critical to the effectiveness of phase 2. It is always preferable that the emulation phase be done in real time (i.e., using synchronous collaborative and communication tools). There are also specific mathematics simulation tools such as the Geometer's Sketchpad (http://www.dynamicgeometry.com/) that the instructor can integrate in a virtual session to facilitate the demonstration, visualization, and enactment of mathematics processes.

In the self-control phase, the third phase of the training model, Sylvia sets up a class wiki and provides several examples of the function domain problem to allow students to practice solving these problems on their own. She also posts a criteria checklist to encourage students to set process- oriented goals related to understanding function domains to help students monitor their progress. In this example, a criteria checklist could consist of prompts in the form of questions such as: (a) Is the function given by a formula or a table? (b) Is the domain of the function specified? (c) Is it possible to graph the function to determine the range? (d) Is it possible to identify patterns from the values provided? In addition, a wiki allows instructors (and students if the instructor wishes) to annotate and edit students' work so that students can see whether or not they are enacting the task processes correctly. A wiki also saves all edit iterations, allowing students (and instructors) to revert to earlier versions so they can monitor progress. Sylvia can also monitor whether or not students have been active on the wiki and send them a personal reminder via e-mail if they have not completed the practice problems. Alternatively, instructors who would like to use LMS features to support the self-control phase can use content creation and delivery tools to set up assignment areas for each student to practice independently the task processes associated with function domain problems. Assignment areas can be public or private. The instructor can also use the course documents feature to post the checklist criteria.

In the self-regulation phase of the four phase training model, students engage in learning function domains independently. Students have now routinized the steps and can turn their attention to outcomes. However, if they commit any errors during their performance they can still use ILT learning tools, specifically exploratory tools such as search tools, to apply different strategies to solve function domain problems. Learning tools provide the opportunity for students to modify strategy use as needed to improve their performance. Students can also use assessment tools (e.g., grading rubrics

TABLE 3.3   An Example of Self-Regulatory Training with ILT

Model phase	Role of student and instructor	ILT
Phase 1—*Observation* • Enable students to think strategically before acting	Student • Observes instructor demonstrating the desired behavior • Takes appropriate notes during the demonstration	Content creation & delivery tools
	Instructor • Identifies the assignment • Performs task analysis • Demonstrates/models the learning task	Collaborative & communication tools
Phase II—*Emulation* • Enable students to gather information about their behaviors and performance with the help of the instructor	Student • Enacts task with instructor/peer support • Demonstrates awareness of goal setting and task strategies • Seeks help when needed	Content creation & delivery tools
	Instructor • Coaches student • Provides feedback	Collaborative & communication tools
Phase III—*Self-Control* • Enable students to focus on mastering the processes related to completing the learning task during practice episodes	Student • Practices task on his or her own • Monitors progress • Rewards progress	Administrative tools
	Instructor • Provides checklist or rubric	Collaborative & communication tools
Phase IV—*Self-Regulation* • Enable students to focus on outcomes and make strategic adjustments when performing poorly	Student • Selects and implements strategies to achieve goals • Modifies strategy use based on outcomes	Learning tools
	Instructor • Available for feedback as needed	Assessment tools

and criteria) to self-evaluate their performance outcomes. Furthermore, if students feel that their performance outcomes are significantly below the outlined criteria, they can contact the instructor using collaborative and communication tools such as e-mail to seek help or obtain elaborative feedback (see Table 3.3 for a depiction of the training model in action).

Conclusion

This chapter provided a description of how college instructors, particularly those who teach remedial freshman courses, can use ILT to promote and support self-regulated learning. Using a four-phase theory-based training model, this chapter described how instructors can use the pedagogical categories and technological features of ILT to train students to become self-regulated learners in online, blended, or distributed learning environments.

References

Ayers, T., Davis, G., Dubinsky, E., & Lewin, P. (1988). Computer experiences in the teaching of composition of functions. *Journal for Research in Mathematics Education, 19*(3), 246–259.

Azevedo, R. (2005). Computer environments as metacognitive tools for enhancing learning. *Educational Psychologist, 40*(4), 193–197.

Azevedo, R., Cromley, J. G., Winters, F. I., Moos, D. C., & Greene, J. A., (2005). Adaptive human scaffolding facilitates adolescents' self-regulated learning with hypermedia. *Instructional Science, 33*(5-6), 381–412.

Bandura, A. (1997). *Self-efficacy: The exercise of control.* New York: W.H. Freeman.

Brooks, D. W. (1997). *Web-teaching: A guide to designing interactive teaching for the World Wide Web.* New York: Plenum Press.

Chang, M. (2007). Enhancing web-based language learning through self-monitoring. *Journal of Computer Assisted Learning, 23*(3), 187–196.

Choi, I., Land. S. M., & Turgeon, A.Y. (2005). Scaffolding peer-questioning strategies to facilitate metacognition during online small group discussion. *Instructional Science, 33*(5–6), 483–511.

Dabbagh, N., & Kitsantas, A. (2004). Supporting self-regulation in student-centered web-based learning environments. *International Journal of e-Learning, 2*(4), 40–47.

Dabbagh, N., & Kitsantas, A. (2005). Using web-based pedagogical tools as scaffolds for self-regulated learning. *Instructional Science, 33*(5-6), 513–540.

Hartley, K., & Bendixen, L. D. (2001). Educational research in the Internet age: Examining the role of individual characteristics. *Educational Researcher, 30,* 22–26.

Henry, M. J. (1995). Remedial math students' navigation patterns through hypermedia software. *Computers in Human Behavior, 11*(3–4), 481–493.

Johnson, D. F. (2003a). Toward a philosophy of online education. In D. G. Brown (Ed.), *Developing faculty to use technology: Programs and strategies to enhance teaching* (pp. 9–11). Hoboken, NJ: Wiley.

Johnson, D. F. (2003b). The ethics of teaching in an online environment. In D. G. Brown (Ed.), *Developing faculty to use technology: Programs and strategies to enhance teaching* (pp. 27–31). Hoboken, NJ: Wiley.

Kauffman, D. F. (2002). *Self-regulated learning in web-based environments: Instructional tools designed to facilitate cognitive strategy use, metacognitive processing, and motivational beliefs.* Paper presented at the annual conference of the American Educational Research Association (AERA), New Orleans, LA.

Kitsantas, A., & Dabbagh, N. (2004). Promoting self-regulation in distributed learning environments with web-based pedagogical tools: An exploratory study. *Journal of Excellence in College Teaching, 15*(1–2), 119–142.

Kramarski, B., & Gutman, M. (2006). How can self-regulated learning be supported in mathematical e-learning environments? *Journal of Computer Assisted Learning, 22*(1), 24–33.

López-Morteo, G., & López, G. (2007). Computer support for learning mathematics: A learning environment based on recreational learning objects. *Computers & Education, 48*(4), 618–641.

Perry, N. E., & Winne, P. H. (2006). Learning from learning kits: gStudy traces of students' self-regulated engagements using software. *Educational Psychology Review, 18,* 211–228.

Prensky, M. (2001). Digital natives, digital immigrants. *On the Horizon, 9*(5). Retrieved June 14, 2007 from: http://www.marcprensky.com/writing/

Salaway, G., Borreson-Caruso, J., & Nelson, M.R. (2007). *The ECAR study of undergraduate students and information technology.* Retrieved January 10, 2008 from: http://connect.educause.edu/Library/ECAR/TheECARStudyofUndergradua/45075

Whipp, J. L., & Chiarelli, S. (2004). Self-regulation in a web-based course: A case study. *Educational Technology Research and Development, 52*(4), 5–22.

Winne, P. H. (2006). How software technologies can improve research on learning and bolster school reform. *Educational Psychologist, 41,* 5–17.

Winne, P. H., Nesbit, J. C., Kumar, V., Hadwin, A. F., Lajoie, S. P., Azevedo, R. A., & Perry, N. E. (2006). Supporting self-regulated learning with gStudy software: The learning kit project. *Technology, Instruction, Cognition and Learning, 3*(1), 105–113.

Zimmerman, B. J. (2000). Attaining self-regulation: A social cognitive perspective. In M. Boekaerts, P. R. Pintrich, & M. Zeidner (Eds.), *Handbook of selfregulation* (pp. 13–39). San Diego, CA: Academic Press.

4

Goal Setting

Contents

Learning to Learn with Integrative Learning Technologies, pages 57–74
Copyright © 2010 by Information Age Publishing

Scenario

You have a gold mine, when you have a goal mind.

Emily is a college instructor who is teaching a large undergraduate remedial algebra course. The students in Emily's class are required by the university to take this course because they did not pass the basic entrance exam in math. Emily is experiencing difficulty in motivating the students to complete the required course assignments. As a result of students' prior negative experiences in mathematics, Emily realizes that her students are convinced that they have poor abilities in math. Consequently, the students lack the motivation and the desire to complete the assignments. Moreover, many students tell Emily that their only goal is to "pass the course."

As the instructor, Emily realizes that in order to help her students succeed in the course she will need to provide them with goals and plans to strategically achieve these goals. Emily decides to help her students set clearly defined, process-oriented goals for all of the course assignments. The course requirements include weekly homework assignments, online quizzes, a midterm, and a final exam. The weekly homework assignments have been designed to offer students a way to practice the problems covered in each chapter of the textbook. The online quizzes include problems from the weekly assignments as well as new problems. Emily explains to her students that they should focus on following specific strategic steps provided to solve the homework problems before taking the online quizzes. The students agree to try and meet this goal and seem to be relieved to have a plan of action.

Additionally, Emily decides to create two collaborative study groups, one online, using the social utility Facebook, and the other face-to-face. Emily announces to students that joining these groups is optional but strongly encouraged, and explains that these groups provide the opportunity for students to receive and share knowledge while working together on the homework assignments.

Emily observes how students are working on the online Facebook group and provides a link to Google Calendar to facilitate student goal setting and monitoring of the group's progress. Emily also develops a goal-setting template for each assignment and makes it available to all students in the course. This template outlines short-term, specific process goals that can guide students to work on course objectives and assignments. After several weeks, Emily sees encouraging results. Students begin to turn in their homework assignments consistently and the online quiz grades begin to rise. Overall, the students seem to have gained confidence in their ability to succeed in passing the course.

What Are Goals?

In educational settings, goals are conceptualized as providing the direction for learner action. A goal may be defined as a desired outcome that the student is consciously trying to attain (Schunk, Pintrich, & Meece, 2008). Specifically, goals provide students with direction on how to act and whether to approach or avoid certain circumstances or tasks. Goals play a key role in a student's motivation to learn and in his or her performance.

From a social cognitive view, goals that are clearly defined, realistic, proximal, and moderately difficult offer the most adaptive motivational benefits. Additionally, process goals, which focus on methods and strategies that can help one master a task, produce better performance and motivation than outcome goals (i.e., goals that focus on outcomes of learning efforts). Students who adopt process goals focus their attention on mastering the strategies to effectively carry out a task. On the other hand, students who select outcome goals focus solely on the end result. The distinction here is that students who adapt process goals are thinking not about the end result but about the different processes that are required to be successful, whereas students who select outcome goals focus ultimately on performance (Zimmerman & Kitsantas, 1999).

Goals have also been distinguished based on mastery (focus on learning), performance-approach (focus on appearing competent), and performance-avoidance (focus on avoiding appearing incompetent) goals. Researchers posit that mastery goals tend to facilitate adaptive outcomes more than performance goals (Schunk et al., 2008). For example, a student who is more mastery oriented would be more intrinsically motivated to learn the content, adopt more process-related goals, use deep-processing strategies, and engage in more adaptive help-seeking behaviors than a student who is simply interested in getting a good grade. In the context of a learning environment, students with a performance-goal orientation set goals that are directly related to specific outcomes of performance, such as achieving high grades and receiving positive judgments from others. These students typically select tasks at which they know they will succeed. Students with a performance-avoidance goal orientation will set goals that prevent them from looking incompetent to others. For example, a student with a performance-avoidance goal orientation consciously procrastinates instead of studying for an exam so when a poor grade is received, he or she can attribute that failure not to his or her own competence, but to an external attribute. On the other hand, performance-goal-oriented students may study for an exam just to show others how capable they are. This typically results in shallower, surface-level processing and study strategies.

In contrast, students who are motivated to gain competence and knowledge are perceived as having a mastery-goal orientation. Students who set mastery goals generally achieve at higher levels than students who set performance goals. Although performance-oriented and mastery-oriented students could be comparable in intelligence and ability, they can be quite different in terms of self-regulatory skills. For example, studies show that students who adopt a mastery orientation toward their goals are more likely than their performance-oriented peers to use self-regulatory strategies and metacognitive skills. In addition, students with a mastery orientation are more likely to persist during challenges while students with a performance orientation could become easily discouraged (Pajares, Britner, & Valiente, 2000; Pintrich, 2000).

The type of goals that students form and construct is influenced by many factors. Specifically, Dembo (2000) suggests that interest, motivation, task difficulty, and competency beliefs will all influence the type of goals that students set as well as their level of commitment to the goals. Assessing motivational beliefs before prompting students to set goals is a constructive approach for educators to take in order to help students set process goals. As an example, many students are motivated by fears of failure (e.g., performance-avoidance goals), rather than by the embrace of success (e.g., mastery goals). Therefore, understanding the relationship or causal paths among student goals, motivational beliefs, and academic achievement is important for designing learning environments that support effective goal setting (Code, MacAllister, Cress, & Nesbit, 2006).

Research on Goal Setting: Implications for Instruction

Effective goals can enhance performance in several ways. First, goals help determine the amount of effort that an individual will expend. Second, goals can help dictate direction, focus, and persistence in a task. And third, goals encourage the use of strategic planning (Locke & Latham, 1990).

However, effective goal setting depends on the type of goals student set (Okun, Fairholme, Karoly, Ruehlman, & Newton, 2006). Students who are mastery-oriented generally (a) view successful achievement as progression and mastery, (b) place more value on effort and academic challenges, (c) feel more satisfied when they have progressed or have actually learned, (d) view errors and mistakes as learning experiences, and (e) view ability as a factor that is malleable and increased through effort. However, students who are more performance-oriented generally (a) view successful achievement as doing better than others, (b) place more value on showing high ability instead of effort, (c) feel more satisfied when they do better than others, (d) view errors and mistakes as lack of ability and failure, and (e) view ability as a fixed entity. These distinctions between mastery- and performance-oriented students influence how students approach tasks, the strategies that they use to accomplish tasks, and ultimately influence the kinds of goals that they set (Schunk et al., 2008).

According to Ames and Archer (1988), student goals can be changed based on what teachers emphasize in the classroom. For example, if instructors emphasize competition among students such as verbally rewarding students for the highest grade, they may be providing cues to students to place more emphasis on performance goals. However, instructors who emphasize learning such as verbally rewarding students for effort may encourage students to set more mastery-oriented goals. Therefore, instructors should reward students for improving performance as opposed to receiving high marks, encourage students to pursue challenging tasks, stress that mistakes are part of the learning process, and discuss with students that ability is a malleable entity that is increased through effort. This approach would likely increase the students' adaptation of mastery-oriented goals and as a result increase strategic learning, motivation, and achievement.

Goal setting has also been associated with attributions. Attributions are the perceived causes of outcomes. Students are likely to attribute their outcomes to a variety of causes both internal (e.g., effort) and external (e.g., luck). Attributions shape the development of students' expectancy beliefs as well as the subsequent affective reactions to events and experiences (Schunk et al., 2008). In the context of *Attribution Theory* (Weiner, 1994, 2000), Weiner posits that most causal explanations relate to three factors. These factors include (1) if the cause is perceived by the individual to be internal or external to the learner, (2) if the cause is perceived to be stable or unstable, and (3) whether or not the cause is controllable.

A central assumption of attribution theory is that individuals tend to attribute successes to internal, stable events, and failures to external factors that were not controllable. The overall explanation for this type of thinking is that individuals have an innate desire to preserve a positive self-image

(Slavin, 2006). In the educational context, attribution theory is applicable in terms of four explanations for causal outcomes for successes and failures. These include luck, ability, task difficulty, and effort. Among these factors, luck and task difficulty are external to the individual, and ability and effort are internal. Specifically, luck is perceived to be unstable and uncontrollable by the learner, whereas task difficulty is perceived as uncontrollable yet relatively stable. In addition, ability is perceived as stable and uncontrollable, whereas effort is perceived as controllable by the learner and could be stable or unstable.

These attributions (i.e., luck, ability, effort, and task difficulty) can have specific influences on a student's goal setting. Importantly, attributions can contribute to the adoption of mastery- or performance-goal orientation. For example, if a student feels that she is able to control her academic success through her effort and ability, she is likely to develop a mastery-goal orientation toward learning. In contrast, a student who feels that she is unable to alter her performance due to internal perceptions of a lack of ability and uncontrollable factors such as luck and task difficulty, will likely give up in the face of obstacles rather than exert more effort. In the latter case, repeated failures can contribute to learned helplessness in the student (Seligman, 1975), which occurs when an individual perceives that failures are caused by factors that are uncontrollable and stable. Students who have developed a learned helplessness orientation tend to set low goals for themselves to avoid failure. For example, a student who has failed a mathematics exam may tell himself or herself that the reason why he or she failed is that he or she is not good at math and just does not have the ability to succeed in the subject (an uncontrollable and stable attribute). As a result, the student feels that there is nothing that can be done to improve the performance. This is where students begin to feel symptoms of depression and passivity and may stop trying to do well by not studying, not paying attention in class, and not doing homework (Schunk et al., 2008).

Researchers (see Schunk et al., 2008) suggest that instructors should be aware of their attributional biases. That is, instructors have been found to often make inaccurate attributions about a disposition or trait in relation to student outcomes. Teachers who believe, based on predispositions (e.g., values, race), that students cannot do well are less likely to implement new instructional activities or engage in other strategies that would increase student achievement. Therefore, Schunk et al. (2008) suggest that although it may be difficult to avoid attributional biases, constantly gathering information about the student may provide teachers with a more comprehensive perspective on the attributes and needs of the student. Instructors can help students attribute failures to controllable factors by emphasizing the role of personal responsibility through student effort and the use of strategies that can serve to promote mastery learning. Toward this end, students can be taught to set small incremental goals, which are attainable and can be measured and rewarded. Research indicates that students who set specific (e.g., "I will learn how to use a word processor") as opposed to general goals (e.g., "I will learn how to use a computer") and process rather than outcome goals show high achievement and motivation for their assigned work (Zimmerman & Kitsantas, 1997; Zimmerman, 2000). Setting process goals will help students realize mini-goals along the way toward achieving more distant or long-term goals. This can help students build confidence and resilience. These types of goals can also help students stay focused during the learning process.

Furthermore, as mentioned earlier, aspects of the instructional environment play a critical role in students' goal setting (Ames & Archer, 1988). More specifically, instructors can do the following to support and promote student goal setting:

- design tasks for novelty, variety, diversity, and student interest;
- encourage students to set specific, realistic, yet challenging goals that are appropriate for them;
- stress the value of improving performance and learning as opposed to comparing one's performance to that of other students in the class;
- teach students to create incentives and self-rewards during the learning process when they achieve particular goals;
- help students identify specific activities and products that they will create to achieve their goals;
- encourage students to set a variety of goals including short- (proximal) and long-term (distal) goals;
- identify potential obstacles that students may face and devise an effective plan of action in response;
- remind students that mistakes are a natural part of the learning process and not an indicator of a lack of ability or intelligence;
- help students view obstacles as temporary setbacks and not lose sight of their goals when setbacks occur;
- ensure students that although the process may be challenging and demanding at times, there will be positive and rewarding outcomes for their commitment in this course and beyond.

The above guidelines can be implemented using a variety of instructional methods in traditional face-to-face learning environments. For example, instructors typically exercise significant control over the learning process in face-to-face classroom settings and are able to monitor student attention and progress closely (Besser & Bonn, 1997). In these contexts, it may be relatively easy for instructors to identify students who lack goal-setting skills. Once those students are identified, instructors can work with them one-on-one to help them set specific goals and select appropriate strategies to attain them. However, in online, blended, or distributed learning environments, learners have an increased responsibility to complete learning tasks on their own and therefore must exercise a high degree of self-regulatory competence to achieve their learning goals. This is partly attributable to the physical absence of the instructor but also to the distributed nature of learning interactions enabled by Integrative Learning Technologies (ILT), as discussed in Chapter 2. Consequently, instructors have an increased responsibility to support and promote self-regulatory strategies to ensure academic success (Kitsantas & Chow, 2007; Kitsantas & Dabbagh, 2004). Next, we provide specific examples of how instructors can use ILT to support the self-regulatory process of goal setting in online, blended, or distributed learning environments.

Supporting and Promoting Goal Setting Using ILT

Overall, research has shown that two ILT categories—collaborative and communication tools and content creation and delivery tools—are most useful in supporting goal setting in online and distributed learning environments (Dabbagh & Kitsantas, 2005; Kitsantas & Dabbagh, 2004). The results of a survey aimed at evaluating how expert instructors utilized ILT to support student self-regulation in online and distributed courses also supported these earlier research results (Dabbagh & Kitsantas, 2009).

Specifically, expert instructors reported using the content module LMS feature (a content creation and delivery tool) to divide the course into manageable modules in order to help students set a learning schedule for each module. This strategy can help students identify specific activities in each module to achieve process goals. Instructors also reported using checklists for every content module to help students set specific dates for beginning and completing each module as well as related assignments. With respect to collaborative and communication tools, instructors reported using the discussion forum to remind students of the course learning objectives and deliverables on a weekly basis and to conduct question and answer sessions to clarify the course requirements so that students can set appropriate process goals. One expert instructor reported using a wiki to help students manage group projects. Wikis have both public and private areas and are a good technology for project management. Instructors also reported using grading rubrics (an assessment tool) to support student goal setting, citing that rubrics helped students set mastery-oriented goals based on the criteria stated in the rubric. Finally, instructors reported using the online calendar (an administrative tool) to keep students abreast of upcoming deadlines, and online portfolios (an assessment and learning tool) to help students set general learning goals at the beginning of the course. Table 4.1 provides additional examples of how instructors can use features from the five ILT categories described in Chapter 2 to implement the goal-setting guidelines identified earlier.

Research has also revealed that using ILT features as instructional prompts to scaffold students in goal-setting exercises is a very effective strategy (Code et al., 2006). Specifically, these researchers are advocating the use of instructional prompts to change a student's attributions from external causes (e.g., luck and task difficulty) to internal causes (e.g., ability and effort), an adjustment that is key in the development of self-regulated learning skills. As discussed earlier in this chapter, attribution theory has particular influences on a student's goal-setting behavior. Hence, it is important that instructors use ILT to train students to attribute academic successes and failures to intrinsic, stable, and controllable factors and to learn how to set motivational personal goals that foster curiosity, learning, personal growth, and self-knowledge. Code et al. (2006) posit that advances in learning technologies are making it possible to scaffold student goal setting in terms of the perceived sense of control and self-efficacy they feel toward a learning task.

In the chapter's opening scenario, Emily's students were convinced that they were poor math students because of their previous failures. They lacked the motivation and the desire to complete the assignments and did not have a plan of action for passing the remedial math course that they had been placed in because of low math grades in high school. Moreover, the students' goal was to pass the course, not to learn math. The instructor was able to use ILT to help the students change their perception of causality for failure from (lack of) ability to ineffective strategy use, and regain control of their learning. In the next section, we present an example of how Emily can use the four-phase training model described in Chapter 3 to train students' goal-setting behavior using ILT.

TABLE 4.1 Examples of Supporting and Promoting Goal Setting Using ILT

Instructional strategies	ILT category	Specific examples
Design tasks for novelty, variety, diversity, and student interest	Content creation and delivery tools (e.g., Web publishing tools and resource sharing tools)	• Embed video snippets that illustrate how the concepts are used in the real world • Select videos that relate to students' interests • Provide a variety of examples to cater for multiple interests
Encourage students to set specific, realistic, yet appropriately challenging goals, as well as a variety of short-term (proximal) and long-term (distal) goals	Administrative tools (e.g., course calendar, course planning and scheduling tools, and student tracking tools)	• Create a weekly online goal setting template specific to the course objectives and requirements to serve as a checklist so that students can set short- and long-term goals • Ask students to keep a personalized calendar and/or a personal tasks journal to keep track of their progress on a daily, weekly, and monthly basis
Stress the value of improvements in personal performance and learning rather than comparing student performance to that of other students in the class	Collaborative and communication tools (e.g., e-mail)	• Send personalized e-mails to each student, commending him or her on their progress and on meeting their goals
Teach students to create incentives and self-rewards during the learning process when they achieve particular goals	Collaborative and communication tools (e.g., social networking tools such as Facebook) Learning tools (e.g., content collection or personalized tools)	• Encourage students to use the gift feature on Facebook to reward themselves after completing a number of goals • Ask students to assign a numerical value to each goal they set using the goal-setting template or personal calendar tool, and use the monthly total of "completed goals" to buy themselves a gift

Instructional strategies	ILT category	Specific examples
Help students identify specific activities and products that they will create to achieve their goals	Learning tools (e.g., content collection or personalized tools)	• Provide information about the variety of online learning tools available to help students create activities to enable them to achieve their goals (e.g., the personal calendar, blogs, and social bookmarking tools)
Identify potential obstacles that students may face and devise an effective plan of action in response	Assessment tools (e.g., online gradebook and online marking tools)	• Conduct an analysis using the online gradebook and online marking tools on tests and assignments to identify common errors or areas of difficulty students are having
	Content creation and delivery tools (e.g., course documents)	• Develop additional materials to assist students in overcoming difficulties using the course documents tool
Remind students that mistakes are a natural part of the learning process and not an indicator of a lack of ability or intelligence	Collaborative and communication tools (e.g., e-mail)	• Send specific e-mails to refocus the student's attention to strategy attribution so that they do not attribute their failures to external causes
Help students view obstacles as temporary setbacks and not to lose sight of their goals when setbacks occur	Content creation and delivery tools (e.g., resource sharing tools)	• Provide students with a link to a video clip that shows how people have overcome obstacles in the real world while achieving an academic goal

Training Students for Goal Setting

In a remedial algebra class, students need to understand how to solve problems like the following: "If $x = -1$ and $y = 2$, what is the value of the expression $2x^3 - 3xy$?" Or, "At, Big Al's restaurant, three cheeseburgers and two orders of fries cost $5.60, but 4 cheeseburgers and three orders of fries cost $7.80. How much does a single cheeseburger and a single order of fries each cost separately?" (http://seattlepi.nwsource.com/local/328864_math24.html). Remedial math students view these problems as a daunting task and have no idea how to get started. The four-phase training model can help instructors use ILT to train students to set incremental and attainable process-oriented goals in order to successfully navigate the terrain of solving such problems and consequently develop controllable attributions that will lead them to become self-regulated and motivated learners.

The math example we will use to illustrate how the model works for supporting and promoting goal-setting strategies is the following: "You are working for Go Green, an environmental agency that tracks the amount of rainfall in different areas of the country. Your boss hands you two pieces of paper. One has a list of daily rainfall data for the first week of April and the other has a list of daily rainfall data for the first week of November. However, when you look at the data for November you notice that the rainfall data for November 7 is missing because someone accidently failed to fill it in and the original sheet cannot be found (see Table 4.2). The questions related to this problem are: How do you express in mathematical symbols and variable names the total amount of rainfall (precipitation) for the first week of any given month? And How do you find the missing piece of information in the November data list?

As an instructor, Emily has already identified the learning task (i.e., the math problem) and performed a task analysis to determine the processes, steps, or procedure associated with performing the learning task. Here are the steps or small exercises that Emily would like students to go through in order to practice the algebraic skills related to solving the math problem.

- Step 1: Write in words how you will determine the total amount of precipitation that fell in the first week of April.
  Answer: "Add together the amount of precipitation that fell on each day in the first week of April. This will give you the total amount of precipitation for the week."
- Step 2: Write in words how you will determine the total amount of precipitation that fell in the first week of November.
  Answer: "Add together the amount of precipitation that fell on each day in the first week of November. This will give you the total amount of precipitation for the week."
- Step 3: Write in words a general description for how you would get the total amount of precipitation for the first week of any given month.
  Answer: "Add together the amount of precipitation that fell on each day of that week. This will give you the total amount of precipitation for that week."

TABLE 4.2 Missing Data

Month/Day	Rainfall	Month/Day	Rainfall
April 1	0.2 ml	November 1	0.5 ml
April 2	1.0 ml	November 2	0.1 ml
April 3	0.0 ml	November 3	0.1 ml
April 4	0.0 ml	November 4	0.2 ml
April 5	0.4 ml	November 5	0.0 ml
April 6	0.0 ml	November 6	0.0 ml
April 7	0.3 ml	November 7	missing data
		Total Precipitation	1.2 ml

Source: Adapted from http://www.jensplanet.com/mathcourse/section3part10.html

- Step 4: Rewrite this general description using mathematical symbols and variables.
  Answer:
  "day1 + day2 + day3 + day4 + day5 + day6 + day7 = total_precipitation" and NOT "day1 + day2 + day5 + day7 = total_ precipitation" or "day1 + day2 + day3 + day4 + day7 = total_precipitation" (a common misconception because of the zero data reported on the days of the week that it did not rain).
- Step 5: Compute the total precipitation for the first week of April.
  Answer: "0.2 + 1.0 + 0.0 + 0.0 + 0.4 + 0.0 + 0.3 = total_precipitation"
- Step 6: Write in words a general description for how you would find the missing piece of information for the last entry of any week.
  Answer: "I would add up the amount of precipitation from the other days (day 1 through day 6), and I would compare this with the amount of total precipitation for the week. I would know that the difference between these two numbers would be the amount that fell on day 7."
- Step 7: Rewrite this general description using mathematical symbols and variables.
  Answer: "day1 + day2 + day3 + day4 + day5 + day6 = the total amount other than day 7" and "total_precipitation − (day1 + day2 + day3 + day4 + day5 + day6) = the amount that fell on day 7."
- Step 8: Compute the missing piece of data for the first week of November.
  Answer: "1.2 − (0.5 + 0.1 + 0.1 + 0.2 + 0.0 + 0.0) = day7"

Basically, Emily came up with these eight steps to help her students set incremental and attainable goals in a step-by-step manner. Emily would like students to use words to verbalize their understanding of the problem and then relate the words to mathematical symbols, variables, and relations, resulting in an algebraic equation. This goal-setting process will help her students concentrate on properly executing these steps and overcome their perception that they are poor math students because of previous failures in math courses.

According to the four-phase model of self-regulatory training, Emily has to first model these steps to her students. How will she do this using ILT? As discussed in Chapter 3 (see Figure 3.1), synchronous communication tools such as the whiteboard feature in an LMS, or a virtual session using Wimba or Adobe Connect are very appropriate for enacting the observation phase. Additionally, Emily should model, and encourage her students to adopt process as opposed to outcome goals. Emily can do these through a virtual session, where she can share with students a PowerPoint presentation in which she models how to break down the math problem into eight steps. Specifically, as Emily models the steps, it would be important for her to use statements such as, "The most important thing for me to understand right now are the concept and processes involved in doing this math problem, before I focus on finding the right answer." As mentioned in Chapter 3, the advantage of using a virtual session or a virtual meeting tool is that students can ask questions in real time because it is a live session. Also, virtual session tools allow instructors to archive the session so that students can view it later at their own convenience. The downside of using a virtual meeting tool is that it is an approximation of a shared space that mixes face-to-face and online practices and although both instructors and students are becoming more familiar with virtual meeting technologies, differences in time zones and hardware and software infrastructure among participants can be troublesome (ELI, 2006).

Alternatively, instructors can use content creation and delivery tools (e.g., preparing a webcast that students can view at their own pace). For example, the instructor can use YouTube, the free Web 2.0 tool, to prepare a video of himself or herself modeling the eight steps associated with the math problem, using a conventional blackboard as if in a face-to-face classroom context. The instructor can upload the video to the course website and ask students to view it and post related comments and questions. In either case, whether using a collaborative and communication tool or a content creation and delivery tool, the goal of the observation phase of the four-phase training model is to encourage students to observe the instructor setting process goals that involve breaking down the math problem into incremental and attainable steps.

Specifically, during the observation phase, Emily's students will be learning through watching the instructor/expert perform the desired task. This aspect of observation can enhance students' learning by providing a visual image for them to emulate. Students' goals during this phase are to effectively observe and note aspects of the process, which they can later use to perform the skill on their own. Learning how to effectively observe an expert modeling a problem-solving process may provide a vehicle for learning transfer beyond the specific goals needed to complete the observed task.

Once students have finished observing the modeled process for solving the math problem, it is time for them to emulate the process in the instructor's presence, which is the emulation phase of the four-phase training model. Synchronous ILT tools are again very appropriate for this phase. The instructor can use virtual meeting tools to set up a virtual session with each student individually or, if it is a large class, the instructor can set up small-group virtual meetings and ask volunteers from each group to emulate the process of breaking down the math problem into eight specific steps to support effective goal-setting strategies.

Alternatively, instructors can ask each student to prepare a video using YouTube to demonstrate how he or she would apply the eight-step process to a similar problem. This is a nonthreatening format that encourages active participation in the learning process. Students feel empowered because they are creating their own content using a Web 2.0 tool, which many educators believe is a valuable learning exercise in and of itself. In addition, this method allows the instructor to provide specific feedback based on each student's performance. The critical issue in this phase is teaching students how to approach solving an algebraic math problem by breaking it into manageable tasks and processes. This will help students build confidence and self-efficacy as they gain mastery of the learning process. The students' goal during the emulation phase is to apply—in the presence of the instructor—the techniques they have observed during the observation phase, so that the instructor can monitor students' use of effective goal setting. Moreover, the instructor should provide insightful feedback in order to promote accuracy and instill motivation for students to perform the new skill on their own later in the learning process.

During the self-control phase, the third phase of the four-phase training model, the instructor should enable students to begin practicing the learning task on their own. This is a critical step toward helping students become self-regulated learners. In the case of the scenario at the beginning of the chapter, Emily created an online group on Facebook to support and promote students' goal-setting during this phase. Facebook supports a learning community model and provides users with a range of tools with which to collaborate and share information. Some educators believe that Facebook can foster identity building and confidence, which is what many of Emily's students need in order to succeed in the course (ELI, 2006).

To support students in the self-control phase, Emily also provided access to required homework problems and asked students to work collaboratively to solve these problems using a similar process to the one she modeled and they emulated. To facilitate the problem-solving process, Emily provided a goal-setting template that models the eight-step process identified in the task analysis. The template is laid out as a checklist, so that students can check off each step as they complete it. Emily also stressed the greater importance of mastering this process over getting the right answer.

Emily can also provide access to Google Calendar so that each student in the group can plan to take the lead on solving a different algebraic math problem. The calendar has a placeholder for lead names and the problems that need to be completed. Students take the lead on a problem and use the goal-setting template to complete the problem-solving steps on their own. Then students can upload the problem solution to the group space and ask for feedback. Emily checks the problem solutions and uses e-mail to guide students who had incorrect solutions to modify their performance by retracing their steps. Emily also drops in on the Facebook group to monitor student progress and is encouraged to see that they are using the goal-setting template to solve the problem. Once students are able to demonstrate that they have mastered their process-oriented goals, Emily turns her attention toward self-regulation, the final phase of the four-phase training model.

In the self-regulation phase, students have mastered the learning task and must now transition from process-oriented goals to outcome goals. In the scenario, Emily's students have developed the ability to solve similar algebraic math problems using the eight-step process. They now need to focus on the solution of algebraic math problems without thinking about the eight-step process. To support this new skill, Emily used ILT assessment tools (e.g., quiz tool) to provide students with a set of math problems similar to the rainfall problem. She emphasized to students via the LMS- announcement feature that their goal is to solve these problems correctly. At this level, the primary sources of motivation will be the students' intrinsic interest in solving the task on their own and their self-efficacy beliefs to effectively solve the math problem. In addition, students can apply the learned skills in relation to goal setting in other courses. Overall, Emily has applied the four-phase model of self-regulation and, through the use of ILT tools, was able to promote in her students effective goal setting, and ultimately, academic success.

Conclusion

This chapter described how instructors of college freshmen can use ILT to support goal setting, a self-regulatory process that helps learners become motivated to learn. The chapter also defined goal setting and emphasized that goals should be specific, proximal, challenging but attainable, measurable, and process-oriented, particularly in the initial stages of learning. In addition, the four-phase training model of self-regulation is discussed to illustrate how instructors can use ILT categories and features to help students set, manage, and achieve their goals within the educational objectives of a course.

References

Ames, C., & Archer, J. (1988). Achievement goals in the classroom: Students' learning strategies and motivation processes. *Journal of Educational Psychology, 80,* 260–267.

Besser, H., & Bonn, M. (1997). Interactive distance independent education: Challenges to traditional academic roles. *Journal of Education for Library and Information Science, 38*(1), 35–42.

Code, J. R., MacAllister, K., Gress, C. L. Z., Nesbit, J. C. (2006). *Self-regulated learning, motivation, and goal theory: Implications for instructional design and e-learning.* Proceedings of the Sixth International Conference on Advanced Learning Technologies (ICALT06), 872–874.

Dabbagh, N., & Kitsantas, A. (2005). Using web-based pedagogical tools as scaffolds for self-regulated learning. *Instructional Science, 33*(5–6), 513–540.

Dabbagh, N., & Kitsantas, A. (2009). *How do experienced online instructors use Integrative Learning Technologies (ILT) to support student self-regulation and learning?* Unpublished manuscript, George Mason University, Fairfax, VA.

Dembo, M. H. (2000). *Motivation and learning strategies for college success.* Mahwah, NJ: Lawrence Erlbaum Associates, Inc.

EDUCAUSE Learning Initiative (ELI). (February, 2006). *7 things you should know about Virtual Meetings.* Retrieved March 23, 2007 from: http://net.educause.edu/ir/library/pdf/ELI7011.pdf

Kitsantas, A., & Chow, A. (2007). College students' perceived threat and preference for seeking help in traditional, distributed and distance learning environments. *Computers and Education, 48*(3), 383–395.

Kitsantas, A., & Dabbagh, N. (2004). Promoting self-regulation in distributed learning environments with web-based pedagogical tools: An exploratory study. *Journal of Excellence in College Teaching, 15,* 119–142.

Locke, E. A., & Latham, G. P. (1990). *A theory of goal setting and task performance.* Englewood Cliffs, NJ: Prentice-Hall.

Okun, M. A., Fairholme, C., Karoly, P., Ruehlman, L. S., & Newton, C. (2006). Academic goals, goal process cognition, and exam performance among college students. *Learning and Individual Differences, 16,* 255–265.

Pajares, F., Britner, S. L., & Valiente, G. (2000). Relation between achievement goals and self-beliefs of middle school students in writing and science. *Contemporary Educational Psychology, 25,* 406–422.

Pintrich, P. R. (2000). The role of goal orientation in self-regulated learning. In M. Boekaerts, P. R. Pintrich, & M. Zeidner (Eds.), *Handbook of self-regulation* (pp. 451–502). San Diego, CA: Academic Press.

Schunk, D. H., Pintrich, P. R., & Meece, J. L. (2008). *Motivation in education: Theory, research, and applications.* Upper Saddle River, NJ: Pearson Education, Inc.

Seligman, M. E. P. (1975). *Helplessness: On depression, development, and death.* San Francisco: W. H. Freeman.

Slavin, R. E. (2006). *Educational psychology.* Boston, MA: Allyn & Bacon.

Weiner, B. (1994). Ability versus effort revisited: The moral determinants of achievement evaluation and achievement as a moral system. *Educational Psychologist, 29,* 163–172.

Weiner, B. (2000). Intrapersonal and interpersonal theories of motivation from an attributional perspective. *Educational Psychology Review, 12,* 1–14.

Zimmerman, B. J. (2000). Attaining self-regulation: A social cognitive perspective. In M. Boekaerts, P. R. Pintrich, & M. Zeidner (Eds.), *Handbook of self-regulation* (pp. 13–39). San Diego, CA: Academic Press.

Zimmerman, B. J., & Kitsantas, A. (1997). Developmental phases in self-regulation: Shifting from process to outcome goals. *Journal of Educational Psychology, 89,* 29–36.

Zimmerman, B. J., & Kitsantas, A. (1999). Acquiring writing revision skill: Shifting from process to outcome self-regulatory goals. *Journal of Educational Psychology, 91,* 1–10.

5

Task Strategies

Contents

Learning to Learn with Integrative Learning Technologies, pages 75–90
Copyright © 2010 by Information Age Publishing
All rights of reproduction in any form reserved.

Scenario

> *Strategies are like recipes: choose the right ingredients, mix them in the correct proportions, and you will always produce the same predictable results.*
> —Charles J. Givens

As an experienced instructor who uses ILT to support teaching a first-year English composition writing course, Xavier assigns students a position paper on the topic of global warming. This is the second in a series of writing assignments aimed at teaching students the basic genres in English composition writing. Xavier's objective for the course is to enable students to understand a writing assignment as a sequence of tasks, including finding, evaluating, analyzing, and synthesizing appropriate original and secondary sources.

In order to help students accomplish these objectives, Xavier designs writing assignments that focus on teaching students how to develop and master persuasive writing skills, or what some call argument writing. Xavier wants his students to learn how to make a claim or take a position regarding an issue and convince the reader of the validity of their claim or viewpoint. As an expert in his field, Xavier knows that if students do not learn argumentation skills early in their college education, they will be ill-equipped to make supported claims in their writing, not only in their first-year English composition course, but in courses across the disciplines as well as in work-related situations.

Xavier is convinced that the topic of global warming will motivate students to take a position and defend it. Furthermore, he wants to teach his students effective task strategies (e.g., take notes, organize resources, review and summarize applicable content), to help them write a clear and competent paper on the topic. Xavier knows that students must be able to know what strategies are most appropriate to use for what task, how to use them, and how to judge whether or not they are effective. Xavier is already using ILT to support teaching and learning in his class, but he would like to use ILT features and tools to specifically support student strategy use so they can master persuasive writing.

What Are Task Strategies?

Task strategies are the tools learners use to self-regulate their learning. According to Schunk and Zimmerman (1998), these strategies can be categorized into either cognitive or affective. Cognitive strategies refer to strategies such as elaboration, organization, and metacognitive strategies that typically result in higher levels of understanding (Schunk, Pintrich, & Meece, 2008). Affective or motivational strategies refer to how students regulate their motivation and self-efficacy beliefs to complete a task (Schunk et al., 2008). It is important that students and instructors think of these two types of strategies not as mutually exclusive but as interrelated, especially when students engage in learning activities.

Specifically, Pintrich (1989) proposed that there is a dynamic and synergistic interplay of learner motivation and cognitive strategies resulting in optimal learning. In fact, Pintrich and Garcia (1991) found that high intrinsic motivation on the part of the learner is associated with deeper and more elaborate use of task strategies relative to learners with low intrinsic motivation. For example, a student who enjoys writing, is efficacious in his or her writing ability, and wants to master the skill, will be more likely to use more effective strategies than a student who has no interest and is less efficacious in writing.

With respect to self-regulation, Schunk and Zimmerman (1998) suggest that cognitive strategies are the result of applying the construct of self-regulated learning in the domain of cognition; however, they also suggest that cognitive strategies can be influenced by applying knowledge and/or beliefs in the domain of motivation. More specifically, the authors recommend that the more skillful self-regulated learners are, the more likely it is that they have more-adaptive motivational beliefs (e.g., mastery goal orientation, high sense of self-efficacy) that result in more effective task strategies.

Task strategies also include surface- and deep-processing strategies. Surface-level strategies are characterized by repetitive reading of the text, vocabulary memorization, and rehearsing. In contrast, deep-processing strategies involve higher cognitive skills such as comprehension monitoring, differentiating between irrelevant and relevant material, and integrating new material into previous knowledge and experience (Nicholls, 1984; Ruban & Reis, 2006). Although there is a clear distinction between surface and deep-processing strategies, it is important to note that in some cases, surface-level strategies can be just as effective as deep-processing strategies. Specifically, a critical component of self-regulated learning is being able to utilize different learning strategies to master the task and to constantly evaluate the effectiveness of the behaviors in achieving the goal (Winne, 1995). As we will discuss later, strategy knowledge is also important in helping the student determine which strategy will work best in which situation. Different academic tasks, such as math exams and reading exams, require different task strategies. For example, rehearsal (e.g., memorization of formulas) may be required in order to achieve a high score on a math test, while summarization may be required to achieve a high grade on a reading comprehension test. Therefore, different study tactics, either deep-processing strategies or surface-level strategies, may be valuable for different types of learning tasks and goals.

Given that there is no doubt that the use of task strategies impacts student achievement, how can instructors promote student use of effective task strategies? To address this question, we review research related to the use of task strategies in academic contexts and the implications of such research for instruction. We also explore specific task strategies that have emerged in the recent literature, which can help students interact meaningfully with the learning content and develop effective study skills.

Research on Task Strategies: Implications for Instruction

Research in the area of self-regulated learning shows that students possess four types of knowledge that could impact effective use of task strategies: domain knowledge, task knowledge, strategy knowledge, and motivational beliefs (Butler & Winne, 1995). These knowledge types can be perceived as dynamic constructs that impact student learning. Specifically, domain-specific knowledge can play a critical role in the types of strategies that students use in the classroom. Studies show a positive relationship between the depth and richness of domain knowledge and effective strategy use. For example, deeper domain knowledge was associated with increased acquisition, use, and transfer of self-regulatory strategies (Butler & Winne, 1995).

Task knowledge on the other hand is developed as a consequence of previous academic experience, which influences subsequent patterns of self-regulation (Butler & Winne, 1995). Learner perceptions regarding a task have also been found to mediate the selection of goals and the strategies utilized by the student to complete the task. Strategy knowledge can be conceptualized as having three characteristics: declarative, which is a description of the strategy, procedural, how to use the strategy, and conditional, when and where to use a particular strategy. Finally, motivational beliefs refer to the beliefs of the individual to effectively control his/her environment, behavior, thoughts, physiological, and affective responses to accomplish a task (Bandura, 1997). Within an academic setting, motivational beliefs influence goal setting, commitment, effort, and persistence during the learning process.

It has been also suggested that learners must be able to know what the appropriate strategies are for the task as well as when, how, and why to use them. These aspects of strategy use are based on the learner's goals, the specific learning tasks, and the educational environment overall. For example, in order for students to successfully self-regulate, they must first know what is self-regulation and the strategies that they must use to effectively engage in it. Second, students must understand how and when to use the strategies. Finally, students must also understand why specific strategies should be used, depending on their academic context (e.g., goals and type of task). Additionally, Schunk et al. (2008) report that strategy value information, which is defined as instruction on the usefulness and benefits of a specific strategy, increases student motivation, encourages students to continue using the strategy, and is related more to achievement than simply instruction in use of the strategy. Therefore, in addition to explaining what, when, why, and how to use a task strategy, it is equally important for instructors to also explain the value and benefits of using task strategies.

Overall, self-regulated learning dictates that students learn to recognize and appropriately apply different strategies according to the nature of the task. The transition from high school to college is a particularly critical period for students and will necessitate the use of higher-level thinking skills and the ability to learn independently (Tuckman, 2003). For these reasons, student success in undergraduate settings is dependent upon the degree to which he or she can effectively apply task strategies to accomplish the academic tasks required. Examples of task strategies that promote active engagement with the learning material include rehearsal strategies, elaboration strategies, organizational strategies, comprehension monitoring strategies, and affective strategies. We elaborate on each of these types of strategies next.

Rehearsal strategies can be thought of as basic memory tasks that involve reciting items and/or verbalizing and visualizing the material to be learned. Use of rehearsal strategies is believed to support the encoding of new information (Stefanou & Salisbury-Glennon, 2002; Weinstein & Mayer, 1986). Examples of rehearsal strategies for basic and complex learning tasks include:

- copying, underlining, or highlighting the learning material;
- clustering, a technique that involves grouping similar material together to enhance recall and conceptual understanding;
- imagery, or visualization techniques that allow the student to create a mental picture or actual graphic of a concept or related concepts; and

- mnemonic devices, which allow the student to organize information by creating stories, rhymes, anagrams, or metaphors to depict the material to be learned.

Elaboration strategies can be perceived as higher-order learning strategies that involve active learner participation to integrate new material with existing knowledge (Ormrod, 2004; Schunk & Zimmerman, 1998; Weinstein & Mayer, 1986). Examples include:

- paraphrasing or summarizing material, a technique in which the student rewrites in his or her own words the information to be learned;
- creating analogies, which involves the comparing of previous learning to a new situation;
- generative note taking, in which the student actively engages in connecting ideas, which is in contrast to passive, linear note taking;
- explaining material to others, also referred to as reciprocal teaching, a method that requires the student to teach others, thereby enhancing his or her own understanding of the material; and
- asking and answering questions, a technique that can be practiced by students either internally (to themselves) or externally (with others) and involves the use of questioning to clarify understanding and comprehension of the material to be learned.

Organizational strategies involve a higher-level process that helps the learner build connections between ideas and structure the material in a meaningful way (Ormrod, 2004; Stefanou & Salisbury-Glennon, 2002; Weinstein & Mayer, 1986). Examples of organizational strategies include:

- outlining text, which can be used by the student to distinguish major topics and ideas;
- creating graphic representations of material, in which learners re-create the material in another format such as a map, pie chart, matrix, time line, or other visual tool; and
- concept mapping, a visualization technique that can be used to relate concepts together providing with a tangible way to ensure accuracy in students' learning.

Comprehension monitoring strategies involve active monitoring by the learner to ensure his or her understanding of the material (Ormrod, 2004;

Weinstein & Mayer, 1986). Examples of comprehension monitoring strategies include:

- self-questioning, or the use of appropriate questions during learning to enhance comprehension;
- using questions at the beginning of a section (i.e., advance organizers) to guide one's reading behavior while studying;
- rereading the learning material to ensure comprehension and check for comprehension failures.

Affective strategies involve helping the learner to create and sustain a learning environment that is conducive to learning (Weinstein & Mayer, 1986). Examples of affective strategies to help students reduce test anxiety include:

- using positive self-talk to reduce anxiety;
- reducing external distractions by studying in a quiet place;
- using thought stopping to prevent or reduce worry about doing poorly on an exam; and
- skipping problematic questions and returning to them later during tests.

The classroom environment plays a critical role in fostering student use of task strategies. For example, instructors who encourage student responsibility and active participation through learning communities can promote student motivation and cognitive engagement, which lead to greater levels of strategy use. This premise was examined in a study by Stefanou and Salisbury-Glennon (2002) with first-semester undergraduate students. In that study the motivational beliefs and strategies of students involved in a learning community were compared to the learning strategies of students not involved in a learning community. The data revealed that students involved in learning communities showed greater use of rehearsal and organization strategies, critical thinking, and time management, and engaged in more peer learning activities and help-seeking behaviors, than students who did not participate in the learning community.

In addition to providing a participatory and collaborative educational climate through learning communities, instructors need to provide specific instruction to learners regarding the use of task strategies. For example, in the case of remedial courses, students are unlikely to understand that their learning can be enhanced through the effective use of task strategies. In response to previous failures, these learners may have developed an attitude of learned helplessness toward learning (Seligman, 1975). Learned helplessness, a state characterized by lack of affect and control, can be perceived as a motivational problem in which students act helpless because they believe that there is nothing they can do to avoid failure (Stipek, 1993). An instructor may help these students increase their self-efficacy beliefs by teaching and modeling the use of effective task strategies. Schunk and Zimmerman (1998) emphasize the instructor's role in modeling effective strategies often, rather than simply providing a single-shot formula, and modeling strategies in response to task demands as they occur. This pattern of instruction can provide opportunities to enrich student learning by illustrating creative applications of strategy use, which may involve modifications and integration of multiple strategies. ILT can play an important role in assisting instructors in demonstrating effective and creative use of task strategies, particularly in remedial and introductory courses that are increasingly reliant on technology to deliver course content and engage students in learning. In the next section, we describe how instructors can use ILT to support effective task strategy use in college freshmen.

Supporting and Promoting Task Strategies Using ILT

The availability of ILT in higher education contexts has created an environment in which task strategies can be placed in the hands of the learner. Technology can empower learners from a tool-using standpoint such that learners can take initiative in determining what strategies to use to meaningfully interact with the learning material (Smith & Ragan, 1993). Clark and Kazinou (2001) posit that learning technologies overall can help prompt students to use different task strategies and that by doing so, students become aware of how they learn. Specifically, technology can help students organize and sequence content, and engage in elaboration and monitoring of understanding (Smith & Ragan, 1993). However, not all students are ready to take control of their own learning, especially students who are in remedial courses or lack self-confidence and self-efficacy. Therefore, instructors must scaffold learners to develop appropriate task strategies using technology to ensure academic success (Dabbagh, 2003).

An example of such scaffolding is the CoNoteS2 tool (Hadwin & Winne, 2001). CoNoteS2 is an electronic notebook designed to support self-regulated learning strategy use through tacit and explicit scaffolding. CoNoteS2 (initially CoNoteS) has three main features: an organizer window that allows students to organize the textbook readings by chapters and chapter sections, a glossary-making tool, and a note-taking tool. Students can also create index terms for highlighted text. All student-created notes and glossaries become hyperlinks for easy access and review. Ultimately, CoNoteS2 is a tool that helps students study strategically by engaging them in self-regulation and encouraging them to use deep-processing strategies (e.g., analyze, summarize, and compare/contrast information) to promote learning and understanding.

Another instructional technology that is very powerful in supporting organizational task strategies is concept mapping. Students can use electronic concept mapping tools such as Inspiration and MindManager to sharpen inference making and critical thinking skills. When used as a preinstruction exercise, concept mapping allows instructors to inspect students' knowledge structures to identify misconceptions and adapt instruction accordingly to facilitate learning (Sonak, McClure, & Suen, 1995). Students can also use concept mapping tools to organize or plan a research paper or group project (Dabbagh, 2001).

With respect to ILT, recent research has revealed that learning tools were most useful in supporting task strategies, followed in importance by content creation and delivery tools and assessment tools (Dabbagh & Kitsantas, 2005). As described in Chapter 2, learning tools can be perceived as tools that enable learners to manipulate content online and hence organize their learning in a meaningful way. Examples of learning tools that can support effective use of task strategies include the ability to (a) annotate text while exploring course content, (b) take notes (online), (c) bookmark and link information, (d) perform a contextualized search, and (e) build a personal folder of relevant course material. Content creation and delivery tools can also support effective use of task strategies. Specifically, this ILT category enables students to demonstrate their understanding of discipline-specific principles through elaboration strategies. Students are able to develop and contribute learning content that synthesizes their knowledge using Web publishing tools, and design complex individual and collaborative course projects that include interactive multimedia elements using resource sharing tools (e.g., Flickr, YouTube and Delicious). Finally, assessment tools allow students to check for comprehension failures through comprehension monitoring strategies. Self-assessments in the form of reflection journals, e-portfolios, or weblogs are particularly useful in supporting comprehension monitoring strategies. Table 5.1 provides a snapshot of how ILT categories and tools can support effective use of task strategies in distributed and online learning environments.

These research findings were also supported in a more recent study (Dabbagh & Kitsantas, 2009) that targeted expert college instructors' ILT use in supporting and promoting student self-regulated learning in online

TABLE 5.1   Task Strategies and ILT Use

Strategy type	ILT category	Specific example
Rehearsal • clustering • imagery • mnemonics • copying, underlining, or highlighting	Content creation and delivery tools	Students use word processors and Web publishing tools to underline, highlight, and cluster learning content
Elaboration • paraphrasing or summarizing material • creating analogies • note taking • explaining material to others	Collaborative and communication tools	Students use online discussion forums to explain the learning material to others, ask and answer questions, and paraphrase and summarize material
• asking and answering questions	Content creation and delivery tools	Students use blogs for generative note taking
Organization • outlining text • creating graphic representations of material • concept mapping	Learning tools	Students use social bookmarking tools such as Delicious to assemble and organize a list of resources relevant to the topic of their assignment Students use LMS glossary tools to build a personal glossary of terms related to a given learning task
Comprehension • self-questioning • rereading • using questions as advance organizers	Assessment tools	Students use self-assessment tools to monitor their understanding of the learning content

and blended courses. Specifically, instructors were asked to provide examples of how they supported nine types of learning strategies using ILT. These included helping students paraphrase and summarize content, relate new knowledge to prior knowledge, organize instructional materials to suit learning needs, review prior tests or assignments to prepare for tests or to complete assigned tasks, work on assignments with other classmates, learn by observing work of other classmates, apply concepts and ideas from lecture notes and readings to other class activities and projects, pull together information from different sources, and understand difficult concepts. Overall, content creation and delivery tools and collaborative and communication tools were most effective in supporting elaboration and organization strategies, whereas learning tools and assessment tools were most effective in supporting rehearsal and comprehension monitoring strategies.

For example, in order to support student use of elaboration and organization strategies that help them integrate newly learned knowledge with preexisting knowledge, instructors reported asking students to find topic-specific web-based articles and post summaries of these articles to the discussion forum (a collaborative and communication tool) in order to engage students in a relevant discussion. Instructors also reported using content creation and delivery tools to post PowerPoint slides with embedded links to readings or videos, and/or directed questions to prompt students' use of deep-processing strategies. In addition, instructors also reported using authentic problems to organize and structure the course content in order to help students build connections among ideas.

With respect to supporting comprehension monitoring and rehearsal strategies, instructors reported using assessment tools to help students actively monitor their understanding of concepts. Specifically, instructors reported providing weekly online quizzes that varied in difficulty in order to motivate students to keep up with the material and prepare for exams. Students received prompt feedback on their quiz responses. Also, instructors reported using interactive online lectures so that students could test their knowledge as they moved through the lecture, prompting students to effectively engage in comprehension monitoring. Finally, instructors reported posting solutions to prior assignments and examples of completed assignments to help students monitor their comprehension as they worked on new assignments.

It is clear from these expert instructors' examples and related research that ILT categories and tools can be very effective in supporting the use of task strategies. However, as mentioned earlier, instructors need not only to support and promote student use of task strategies but also to guide students to identify (1) what specific strategy they can use for a given learning task, (2) when to use a particular strategy, (3) why a particular strategy is appropriate for a given learning task, and finally (4) how students can use a strategy to perform or accomplish the assigned task. In the next section, we use the chapter scenario to provide a more specific illustration of how instructors can use ILT to train students to use effective task strategies in order to help them become self-regulated learners and ensure academic success.

Training Students to Use Task Strategies

ILT have consistently played a major role in supporting and facilitating writing skills. Starting with the word processor, which revolutionized the editing process, and moving to text-based collaborative and communication tools, which enable anyone with computer and Internet access to express his or her viewpoints and receive related comments, no English composition class is complete without integrating technology to support effective writing strategies. Selfe (1999) argued that instructors can no longer afford to deny the carefully constructed link between literacy and technology. Xavier, the instructor in the scenario at the beginning of this chapter, realizes the importance of this link. Xavier also realizes that the writing process has become an integral part of this new technological world. Using the four-phase training model (observation, emulation, self-control, and self-regulation), Xavier begins to use ILT to design the writing assignments in his course to support students' application of task strategies. Xavier wants to teach his students how to develop an argument by making a claim, providing evidence to support the claim, and crafting a piece of writing that is college level. In preparation, Xavier begins by performing a task analysis for designing the learning task and consults several software technologies that support this writing process.

The task analysis reveals that he will first need to provide students with an overview of argument or persuasive writing techniques in order to reveal the components of this writing genre, which include (a) making a valid claim, (b) finding evidence to support this claim, and (c) constructing qualifiers and rebuttals. In order to provide this overview, Xavier builds a list of web-based resources that provide examples of this writing genre using content creation and delivery tools. In essence he is modeling this writing process by providing examples of how seasoned writers prepare draft outlines, organize their writing resources, and synthesize the information into a coherent argument. Xavier uses Delicious, the resource sharing and tagging tool, to provide best-practice examples of argument writing. He wants his students to be able to distinguish among the different types of claims used in argument writing (e.g., claims of value, claims of cause, and claims of policy). He selects examples that include visual elements (e.g., audio clip or video clip) to help the students understand the concept of claims across media.

Next, Xavier uses concept mapping software (e.g., Inspiration) to develop a visual outline (flowchart) of argument-writing style, providing students with the main sections and subsections of writing an argument and how these sections connect. Then he uses Google Docs (a content creation and delivery tool) to provide this outline in text form and annotates the text to articulate what each section in the outline signifies. In essence, Xavier is modeling effective use of rehearsal strategies (highlighting through annotation) and organizational strategies (outlining, graphic representations, and concept mapping) that support the argument-writing process using ILT. In turn, students are observing the use of these task strategies in relation to argument writing, which is what happens in the observation phase of the four-phase model.

In the emulation phase of the four-phase model, Xavier posts three short writing assignments on Google Docs that require students to analyze particular claims based on the outline and resources he provided in the observation phase. Then he asks groups of students to select three of the argument-writing resources posted on Delicious and to analyze these resources using the advance organizers he created in the observation phase (i.e., the flowchart and outline of the argument-writing process). This technique prompts students to monitor their understanding of the specific procedure or steps involved in writing an argument. He also asks students to use ILT learning tools that support rehearsal and organizational strategies, particularly highlighting, outlining, annotating, and clustering. Since students are completing this task using Google Docs, Xavier can easily provide feedback and coach them. Google Docs allows collaborative editing and saves all drafts so that both students and the instructor can revisit previous drafts as needed to monitor their learning.

Next Xavier sets up a wiki, a content creation and delivery tool, so that students can collectively blog about the main writing topic of this assignment. Xavier wants each student to take a position on global warming to enable him or her to write on the topic. In other words, he wants each student to make a claim and provide credible evidence to support that claim. Additionally, Xavier's goal is for each student to complete this assignment without direct coaching, to enable the self-control phase of the four-phase model. He wants students to focus on mastering the processes related to completing an argument paper and to understand that a writing assignment is a series of tasks that include finding, evaluating, analyzing, and synthesizing appropriate primary and secondary sources. More important, he wants students to understand that in order to complete these tasks, use of appropriate task strategies is essential. Focus on the strategies may prompt students to attribute academic outcomes to more internal and controllable causes such as strategy use. If so, they will advance their own sense of efficacy and motivation to learn. Xavier encourages students to use Delicious to collect and organize their primary and secondary resources. He also asks students to read each other's blogposts and provide comments to promote comprehension monitoring of the argument writing style.

Finally, Xavier uses assessment tools to engage students in phase four of the training model—self-regulation. Specifically, Xavier develops an online self-assessment tool that allows students to test their knowledge of argument writing by evaluating their position or claim on global warming using the self-assessment criteria. Students' use of task strategies is now routinized and therefore, students' attention can be shifted toward performance outcomes. In summary, by applying the four-phase training model, Xavier has been able to use ILT tools and features (content creation and delivery tools, learning tools, and assessment tools) to specifically support student strategy use so they can master the skills of persuasive writing.

Conclusion

This chapter described the role of task strategies in self-regulated learning. It also provided guidelines on how instructors can use ILT to help students select and use appropriate task strategies in order to successfully complete a learning task and consequently feel empowered and motivated to learn. Using a variety of task strategies helps students structure their learning environment, organize learning tasks, and increase their self-efficacy beliefs. Instructors can train students to become strategic learners by teaching and modeling the use of task strategies using ILT in order to help learners replace ineffective strategies with more effective ones.

References

Bandura, A. (1997). *Self-efficacy: The exercise of control.* New York: W. H. Freeman & Co.

Butler, D. L., & Winne, P. H. (1995). Feedback and self-regulated learning: A theoretical synthesis. *Review of Educational Research, 65,* 245–281.

Clark, R. & Kazinou, M. (2001). *Promoting metacognitive skills among graduate students in education.* Retrieved June 20, 2002 from: http://et.sdsu.edu/RClark/ET640/RCMKPOPS2.htm

Dabbagh, N. (2001). Concept mapping as a mindtool for critical thinking. *Journal of Computing in Teacher Education, 17*(2), 16–23.

Dabbagh, N. (2003). Scaffolding: an important teacher competency in online learning. *TechTrends for Leaders in Education and Training, 47*(2), 39–44.

Dabbagh, N., & Kitsantas, A. (2005). Using web-based pedagogical tools as scaffolds for self-regulated learning. *Instructional Science, 33*(5-6), 513–540.

Dabbagh, N., & Kitsantas, A. (2009). *How do experienced online instructors use Integrative Learning Technologies (ILT) to support student self-regulation and learning?* Unpublished manuscript, George Mason University, Fairfax, VA.

Hadwin, A., Winne, P. (2001). CoNoteS2: a software tool for promoting self-regulation. *Educational Research and Evaluation, 7,* 313–334.

Nicholls, J. G. (1984). Achievement motivation, conceptions of ability, subjective experience, task choice, and performance. *Psychological Review, 91,* 328–346.

Ormrod, J. E. (2004). *Human learning* (4th ed.). Upper Saddle River, NJ: Pearson-Merrill Prentice-Hall.

Pintrich, P. R. (1989). The dynamic interplay of student motivation and cognition in the college classroom. In C. Ames & M. L. Maehr (Eds.), *Advances in motivation and achievement: Motivation enhancing environments* (Vol. 6, pp. 117–160). Greenwich, CT: JAI Press.

Pintrich, P. R., & Garcia, T. (1991). Student goal orientation and self-regulation in the classroom. In M. L. Maehr & P. R. Pintrich (Eds.), *Advances in motivation and achievement: Goals and self-regulatory processes* (Vol. 7, pp. 371–402). Greenwich, CT: JAI Press.

Ruban, L., & Reis, S. M. (2006). Patterns of self-regulatory strategy use among low-achieving and high-achieving university students. *Roeper Review, 28,* 148–156.

Schunk, D. H., Pintrich, P. R., & Meece, J. L. (2008). *Motivation in education: Theory, research, and applications.* Upper Saddle River, NJ: Pearson-Merrill Prentice-Hall.

Schunk, D. H., & Zimmerman, B. J. (Eds.). (1998). *Self-regulated learning: From teaching to self-reflective practice.* New York: The Guilford Press.

Selfe, C. (1999). *Technology and literacy in the twenty-first century: The importance of paying attention.* Carbondale: Southern Illinois University Press.

Seligman, M. E. P. (1975). *Helplessness: On depression, development, and death.* San Francisco: W.H. Freeman.

Smith, P. L., & Ragan, T. J. (1993). *Instructional design.* Upper Saddle River, NJ: Prentice-Hall.

Sonak, B., McClure, J., & Suen, H. (1995, October). *A comparison of concept mapping scoring methods.* Paper presented at the Northeastern Educational Research Association (NERA) Annual Meeting, Ellenville, NY.

Stefanou, C. R., & Salisbury-Glennon, J. D. (2002). Developing motivation and cognitive learning strategies through an undergraduate learning community. *Learning Environments Research, 5,* 77–97.

Stipek, D. J. (1993). *Motivation to learn: From theory to practice* (2nd edition). Needham Heights, MA: Allyn and Bacon.

Tuckman, B. W. (2003). The effect of learning and motivation strategies training on college students' achievement. *Journal of College Student Development, 44,* 430–437.

Weinstein, C. E., & Mayer, R. (1986). The teaching of learning strategies. In M. Wittrock (Ed.), *Handbook of research on teaching and learning* (pp. 315–327). New York: Macmillan.

Winne, P. H. (1995). Inherent details in self-regulated learning. *Educational Psychologist, 30*(4), 173–187.

6

Self-Monitoring and Self-Evaluation

Contents

Learning to Learn with Integrative Learning Technologies, pages 91–108
Copyright © 2010 by Information Age Publishing
91

Scenario

> *Follow effective action with quiet reflection. From the quiet reflection will come even more effective action.*
>
> —Peter F. Drucker

Nadia is the instructor of an undergraduate introductory computer science course. The course introduces students to basic computer science concepts and prepares them to be successful in subsequent and more advanced courses. Nadia notices differences among her students, especially between Sarah and John. The differences between these two students are striking, in terms of their ability to keep track of their academic learning tasks and engage in self-reflective practices. As an example, Sarah arrives to class on time and sits in the front row, while John is frequently late and slides into a chair at the back of the class. Sarah is responsive to questions the professor poses during instruction and appears to be listening attentively and writing notes. Sarah asks questions about assignments that are due and carefully records progress that she is making to complete these assignments. John, on the other hand, seems distracted, and it is unclear whether he is taking notes or doing other activities on his laptop, which is always in front of him. In addition, Sarah has one of the highest grades in the class due to her well-thought-out programming assignments and her performance on tests and quizzes. John turns in assignments late, if at all, and his assignments lack structure and coherence. Furthermore, his test and quiz grades are generally below the class average.

Clearly, Sarah is an example of a self-regulated student, whereas John seems to coast through the class without direction or focus. As the instructor, Nadia recognizes that Sarah is employing self-monitoring and self-evaluation processes that help keep her on track. Nadia also realizes that John and others in her class could greatly benefit from using these processes. Therefore, she decides to incorporate self-monitoring and self-evaluation into future lesson plans. She begins thinking about what she can do to promote self-reflective practices. Nadia's first step is to help students reflect upon their classroom habits and study skills and how these habits may be affecting their performance. She begins by developing a checklist that supports and promotes student thinking about planning, monitoring, and evaluating performance on learning tasks and course assignments. Next, she develops a step-by-step procedure in an outline and a visual format to help students follow specific steps when writing a computer program. Finally, Nadia develops a self-assessment protocol that prompts students to evaluate their performance on practice tests. The protocol includes directives to review incorrect responses and correct them. As an incentive, Nadia awards additional points to students who complete the assessment protocol in a timely manner. It is Nadia's hope that these techniques will encourage students like John to reflect upon their performance and take responsibility for their own learning.

What Are Self-Monitoring and Self-Evaluation?

Self-monitoring and self-evaluation are key processes of self-regulation and are essential to a learner's ability to effectively regulate cognitive processes (Schraw, 1998; Zimmerman, 2008). Generally, self-monitoring is related to one's own awareness of comprehension and performance during the learning process, and self-evaluation involves the ability to reflect upon one's performance outcomes and aspects of the learning process (Kitsantas & Zimmerman, 2006; Schraw, 1998; Zimmerman, 2008). Learners who take the initiative to engage in self-monitoring and self-evaluation become aware of their learning process by observing or monitoring their learning and subsequently analyzing and making evaluative judgments about their learning behavior. These processes continuously improve understanding and performance.

Self-Monitoring

Self-monitoring, also labeled as self-observation (Schunk & Zimmerman, 1998), is the process by which students observe, measure, and record their own progress. It involves students questioning themselves about how the task strategy in use has helped or not helped them progress toward their desired goal and how much effort their approach to learning requires (Pressley & Ghatala, 1990). It has been suggested that in many cases, simply recording a particular behavior is a critical aspect of student learning, motivation, and academic success (Zimmerman & Kitsantas, 2005; Zimmerman, 2000). For example, Zimmerman (1995) reports that self-monitoring can enhance self-efficacy beliefs in students through the improvement of student control of the learning process. This in turn prompts the development of intrinsic motivation for independent learning. Thus, teaching students to self-monitor their own progress can promote learner independence, which is relevant for students of all ages, particularly at the undergraduate level.

According to Zimmerman (1999), there are three aspects of self-monitoring. These include monitoring associated with self-evaluation, monitoring of strategy implementation, and monitoring of outcomes to adjust strategies. These three aspects of self-monitoring are deliberately enacted by students to guide their behavior toward successful goal attainment. Based on these aspects of self-monitoring, students would evaluate their monitored progress and outcomes against either a personal or an external standard, monitor how effective the strategy is in helping them achieve a goal, and determine how to adjust strategy use to achieve the goal. All aspects of monitoring, evaluating, and adapting are cyclically related because they influence, inform, and interact with one another. Thus, self-monitoring is a critical process of self-regulated learning because it allows students to be aware of their thought processes and learning behaviors and how these practices can be changed to facilitate adaptive outcomes.

In summary, self-monitoring can serve as a guide for students to become aware of all aspects of themselves as learners, as well as aspects of the learning environment. In this way, students who use information gleaned from self-monitoring to effectively structure their environment can modify behavior to meet their goals.

Self-Evaluation

Self-evaluation is one of the components of the self-reflection phase of Zimmerman's three-phase model of self-regulation discussed in Chapter 1. Self-evaluation refers to how students personally assess their capabilities and progress. It is related to self-judgments learners make based on self-monitored outcomes. For example, when a student receives the results from a test, he or she will first judge the feedback by comparing the current performance to the expected performance, then decide on subsequent actions and efforts.

Students make self-evaluative judgments in one of four ways (Zimmerman & Kitsantas, 2005): by applying a mastery criterion, which is an absolute evaluative standard that has been created by an expert in the specific area of performance; by comparing current performance with one's previous performance; by relying on evaluative criteria based upon a normative standard, which compares performance to other students, rather than an absolute standard; and by using a collaborative standard, which involves participation in a group effort. In the last case, the learner assesses performance according to whether or not he or she has fulfilled the responsibilities defined by the group. Engaging in these self-evaluative judgments assists the students in deciding whether to continue with the specific task strategy or abandon it and adopt another, more effective strategy.

Researchers have also distinguished between two levels of evaluative judgments that promote self-regulated learning: absolute standards and graduated standards (Kitsantas & Zimmerman, 2006). Whereas absolute standards for difficult tasks lead to simplistic, rigid interpretations of performance outcomes (i.e., pass or fail), which can be discouraging, graduated standards provide the learner with greater flexibility in terms of evaluation. For example, graduated standards are sensitive to minor improvements in performance over time that can promote adaptive changes when performance is perceived to be lacking. To promote learner confidence and self-efficacy, positive evaluations based on small improvements can occur along the way. In fact, expert learners have been found to evaluate and modify task strategies to achieve their goals. Therefore, in order for self-evaluation to be more effective, students should be encouraged to use graduated standards for comparison.

Overall, self-evaluation has been posited as a critical process of self-regulation. Self-regulated learners proactively and consistently evaluate their performance. They compare their performance to previous performances or to explicit or implicit standards to reveal knowledge gaps and to modify their behavior accordingly.

Research on Self-Monitoring: Implications for Instruction

Effective self-monitoring may result in behavior change. However, for this to occur, the learner must have the ability to recognize the desired outcome and whether it has occurred, and record and reflect systematically on the result of that assessment. For example, students need to set a goal for what they want to achieve and then be able to reflect on and react to possible discrepancies with actual achievement. Students who are instructed to record their progress systematically (e.g., after every test students fill out a worksheet that questions their reactions and judgments and what they can do in the future to improve) will be more likely to increase future performance and adopt more-adaptive beliefs and behaviors. Additionally, Butler and Winne (1995) suggest that effective self-monitoring is dependent upon feedback and goal setting. In addition, other factors of self-regulated learning such as motivational beliefs and task strategies also need to be promoted and taught in order for students to reap the benefits of self-monitoring (Lan, 1996). Therefore, simply teaching students how to self-monitor is not enough to substantially improve their academic performance (Gynnild, Holstad, & Myrhaug, 2008). The nature of self-regulated learning, after all, is a cyclical process involving several factors that interact and influence one another.

In order to effectively teach self-monitoring to students, instructors must clearly articulate and demonstrate the behavior to be monitored, the monitoring behavior, and the recording system to be used (e.g., keeping track of numbers, graphing). Toward this end, the instructor will utilize rehearsal, modeling, testing, and reviewing to ensure accuracy of self-recording (Schunk & Zimmerman, 1998). In addition, the instructor must coach students in how to handle (i.e., problem solve) situations that may arise that have not been covered in class.

In relation to the scenario at the beginning of this chapter, John is a college student who is having difficulty staying on task. Nadia, the class instructor, realizes that John can benefit from self-monitoring techniques. Specifically, these techniques can help John increase on-task behaviors while encouraging personal responsibility through self-reflective practice. Vanderbilt (2005) has identified ten key steps for implementing self-monitoring in the classroom. The steps are:

1. Identify the problem behavior or academic area of concern.
2. Define the target behavior and develop a replacement behavior.
3. Collect baseline data on the behavior (record how often the behavior is occurring and the extent to which is it interfering with the student's learning).
4. Schedule a conference with the student to discuss the problem and to convince the student that he or she would benefit from adhering to a self-monitoring program.
5. Select self-monitoring procedures.
6. Teach the student to use self-monitoring procedures.
7. Have the student implement the self-monitoring procedures.
8. Use specific verbal praise.
9. Monitor student progress.
10. Perform maintenance and follow-up.

John also has problems with arriving to class on time, turning in assignments on time (if at all), asking appropriate questions in class, and recording important information. It is also unclear whether he is taking notes in class. Nadia knows that John's grades are below the class average, so it is clear that John's off-task behavior is interfering with his learning. According to Vanderbilt (2005), the next step in such a situation is to schedule a conference with John to discuss his behavior and convince him that a self-monitoring program would greatly benefit him (step 4). However, it is sometimes very difficult for college instructors to devote personal attention to every student who exhibits poor self-monitoring behaviors, especially in large college classes and in classes that are increasingly using Integrative Learning Technologies (ILT). Thus the question is, How can a college instructor support and promote student self-monitoring skills using ILT?

Supporting and Promoting Self-Monitoring Using ILT

Overall, research has revealed that administrative tools (e.g., course planning and scheduling tools such as the online course calendar), and assessment tools (e.g., student portfolios and the online gradebook) (see Chapter 3) are more effective in supporting student self-monitoring than other ILT categories and tools (Dabbagh & Kitsantas, 2005; Kitsantas & Dabbagh, 2004). Additionally, these findings were further supported by the results of a more recent study (Dabbagh & Kitsantas, 2009) that targeted expert college instructors' ILT use in promoting student self-regulation skills in online and blended courses.

Specifically, with respect to self-monitoring, instructors were asked to provide examples of how they used ILT to support and promote three key self-monitoring strategies: helping students (a) keep track of their progress on assignments; (b) check their grade on an assignment, quiz, or test; and (c) stay current or up-to-date on class assignments and due dates. The results revealed that the grades tool, which belongs in the ILT assessment category, was the most frequently used to promote student self-monitoring by the instructors. This was followed by the assignment tool, which belongs in the ILT content creation and delivery category, the calendar tool (ILT administrative category), and e-mail (ILT collaborative and communication category). Table 6.1 provides specific examples of how college instructors used these tools to support student self-monitoring.

Research on Self-Evaluation: Implications for Instruction

Self-evaluation of progress or competence has been shown to be a powerful aspect of student learning. Studies have reported that self-evaluation is more more influential on student self-efficacy and self-regulation when learning goals are also present (Schunk & Ertmer, 1999). Specifically, Schunk and Ertmer found that students who focused on process goals made higher self-evaluations about themselves than students who focused on performance goals. Additionally, research has shown that more-frequent self-evaluation leads to higher self-efficacy beliefs and more adaptable and controllable attributions, such as poor strategy implementation (Zimmerman, 2000).

However, most students will not voluntarily engage in self-evaluation. Therefore, teachers must encourage students to periodically monitor and

TABLE 6.1   Using ILT to Support Self-Monitoring

Self-monitoring strategies	Examples of ILT use to support self-monitoring
Helping your students keep track of their progress on assignments	• "Using the grade tool of the Learning Management System (LMS), I consistently post the points a student has earned on an assignment, the possible total score, the class average for that assignment, and the overall cumulative score." • "I use the WebCT assignment tool. For some assignments, I divide assignments into two parts—a draft and a revised version."
Helping your students check their grades on an assignment, test, or quiz	• "I e-mail each student to inform him or her of course progress to date." • "I use the My Grades function in the LMS. Any time a piece of work is graded, it is posted almost immediately so students know where they stand at all times in the course." • "I use the grading tool to post all grades for all classes. Assignment grades and exam grades are posted within two days of submission." • "I use the standard LMS gradebook options. Students can click on grades and see their grade. I also send out an e-mail to each student individually with feedback, at least for the project assignments (not for the discussion assignments)."
Helping your students stay current on class assignments and due dates	• "The syllabus is posted online; it contains a timeline for assignments." • "Courses are divided into modules. For every module, I use checklists where students identify a learning schedule and set specific dates for completion of each assignment as well as beginning and completion of each module. In addition, a course progress page is accessible to each student at any time. The mentor/instructor maintains this progress page, which also displays the checklist dates set by the student. Assignments are marked off as completed and cumulative grades and module feedback notes are entered by the mentor." • "I use the announcements feature and the calendar feature in the LMS." • "I use the assignment tool in Moodle (an LMS) which automatically puts the due dates in the calendar. I also send out e-mails to the whole class as reminders." • "I use the WebCT (LMS) calendar tool, posted syllabus, and grade tool to reinforce deadlines." • "I use the assignments tool in WebCT." • "I use the online calendar to post the assignments and due dates."

evaluate their progress. Researchers suggest several ways that instructors can ensure that students are effectively self-evaluating (Schunk et al., 2008). These include:

- stating clear evaluative standards and criteria to students;
- providing techniques to students to monitor goal progress toward these standards on a regular basis;
- encouraging students to self-reward for making progress toward their goals;
- encouraging students to evaluate progress based on their own performance rather than in comparison to others; and
- providing students who are not progressing toward their goals with support in the form of study groups and online support.

As mentioned earlier, instructors teaching large classes and/or blended and online courses will encounter difficulties helping students on an individual basis assess progress using traditional face-to-face techniques. ILT can help instructors support and promote student self-evaluation in multiple ways. This is discussed next.

Supporting and Promoting Self-Evaluation Using ILT

Overall, research has revealed that ILT content creation and delivery tools and assessment tools were reported as particularly useful for student self-evaluation (Dabbagh & Kitsantas, 2005; Kitsantas & Dabbagh, 2004). Additionally, the results of these research studies revealed that students found content creation and delivery tools useful in scaffolding self-evaluation while completing assignments involving problem-solving tasks. These findings were further supported by the results of a more recent study (Dabbagh & Kitsantas, 2009) that targeted expert college instructors' ILT use in promoting student self-regulation skills.

Specifically, these expert instructors were asked to provide examples of how they supported four key self-evaluation strategies using ILT: helping students (a) check over their work to make sure they did it right, (b) judge how well they are doing in the course, (c) stay apprised of the course's learning objectives, and (d) receive feedback on an assignment. Overall, a checklist (content creation and delivery tools category) was the most frequently used method to support self-evaluation. Next, instructors used the grades tool (assessment category), followed by e-mail (collaborative and communication category) and by online rubrics created and posted using ILT content creation and delivery tools. See Table 6.2 for examples.

TABLE 6.2   Using ILT to Support Self-Evaluation

Self-evaluation strategies	Examples of ILT use to support self-evaluation
Helping your students check over their work to make sure they did it right	• "Learners submit work to mentor; mentor reviews work, writes suggestions, identifies needs for change or extension; returns edited work to learner by e-mail; cycle continues until learner and mentor feel the best product related to the assignment has been constructed." • "The embedded questions in the online lecture give immediate feedback and let students go back to review material they missed." • "Students are provided with a detailed checklist of what is expected. Students check their work using a code validation. If they follow the checklist and validate the code, they will be evaluating the project in exactly the same way that I will." • "Students are provided with online rubrics with each assignment."
Helping your students judge how well they are doing in the course	• "Encourage students to write reflections." • "Grades are posted quickly." • "Assignments are submitted online, allowing for brief written feedback for each student." • "Instructor provides feedback through e-mail." • "The WebCT grade tool allows students to see their grades." • "Students can check grades online."
Helping your students stay apprised of the course's learning objectives	• "Each LMS module begins with learning objectives; students may review this material whenever they wish." • "The syllabus is posted and updated as needed." • "For each assignment, I give a purpose (objective) and then explain how to do the assignment." • "WebCT provides multiple means of reinforcing learning objectives through posted syllabi, self-tests, and study guides." • "I use the syllabus tool in WebCT." • "Course objectives are posted as part of the syllabus."
Helping your students receive feedback on an assignment	• "I use track changes in Word to provide feedback on a writing assignment." • "I use e-mail, synchronous chat, and the course progress page." • "Comments are presented to students via the assignment tool on Blackboard." • "I communicate with students through individual e-mails, not through the ILT/LMS interface. But I do get their e-mail addresses from the interface, and click on them, which opens up my personal e-mail program."

Self-evaluation strategies	Examples of ILT use to support self-evaluation
	• "The WebCT Upload tool has a feedback box, where I give comments."
	• "Occasionally, we'll do group work via a wiki, and I may give very brief feedback via assignments in WebCT. Most comments are made inline in the medium in which the students are working."
	• "I use macros for grading papers and providing extensive feedback on common problems."

Training Students to Become Self-Reflective Learners

We return now to the chapter scenario in which Nadia, the instructor of an introductory computer science course, is concerned about her students' ability to engage in self-reflective practice. This section describes how Nadia can use ILT to incorporate the four-phase training model discussed in Chapters 1 and 3 to enhance self-monitoring and self-evaluation in students who, like John, are having difficulty in these areas. Nadia presents a computer programming problem, which she often gives as an assignment: "Write a C program that will print out all the prime numbers between 3 and 100." She creates a self-reflective practice checklist (see Table 6.3) to model for students how to successfully complete this programming assignment using planning, monitoring, and evaluation strategies. She decides to model how to solve the problem using a synchronous virtual session in which she shares a PowerPoint (PPT) presentation that portrays the phases and steps of the checklist. During the live virtual session, she verbally walks students through the presentation and records the whole session so that students can access the presentation at any time online. Nadia wants to demonstrate the following in the observation phase: (a) the behavior to be monitored, (b) the monitoring behavior, and (c) the recording system to be used to keep track of progress.

First Nadia demonstrates how she determined the algorithm (a blueprint for a computer program) associated with solving the assigned computer programming problem. She poses aloud the four questions of the planning process (see Table 6.3). She verbalizes this as follows: "For example, in answer to the question what is my goal? I will set the following process goals when encountering a problem like this: (a) I want to write out what I know about prime numbers (e.g., definition division), (b) I want to write out the process of figuring out how to determine whether the inte-

TABLE 6.3   A Self-Reflective Practice Checklist

Self-regulatory process	Example of learning task or assignment
Planning	
1. What is the task?	1. Develop a computer programming algorithm (problem solving)
2. What is my goal?	2. Break down the task into steps.
3. What strategies would be most effective to help me complete the task?	3. Study the instructor's virtual session and record the procedures that depict the algorithm. Additionally, form a flowchart that converts the steps to a logic flow and annotate the steps that require repeat and decision logic
4. How should I manage my time, and do I need any additional resources?	4. Establish a baseline to determine time needed to write the algorithm and identify task-related resources provided by the instructor
Monitoring	
1. Am I clear on what steps I need to take?	☐ Yes ☐ No ☐ Not Sure
2. Do I understand the task?	☐ Yes ☐ No ☐ Not Sure
3. Are my goals being successfully achieved?	☐ Yes ☐ No ☐ Not Sure
4. If I checked No or Not Sure to any of these questions, then what changes do I need to make?	
Evaluating	
Have I successfully achieved my goal? If yes what facilitated or hindered my performance?	☐ Yes ☐ No

ger is a prime number using a correct algorithm, and (c) I want to map C language to the procedure." Next Nadia demonstrates how to break down the problem into two main steps: "(1) We need to recall the definition of a prime number, which is 'an integer that can be divided *only* by 1 and itself to leave no remainder,' and (2) we need to understand what this definition means by breaking it into further components to avoid ambiguity because an algorithm must be 'unambiguous'." Nadia also proceeds to identify three distinct components to writing this algorithm: first, the algorithm involves only integers; second, the algorithm involves integer division; and third, the algorithm involves examining the remainder from an integer division to determine whether or not something can be exactly divided by a number.

Nadia wants her students to think carefully about how to implement these three distinct components to write a successful algorithm. She gets more specific. She tells students that implementing these steps involves picking an integer between 3 and 100, and checking if this integer is a prime number using the three attributes of the definition she outlined. She demonstrates this by saying, "For example, if you pick 61, you want to begin dividing 61 by small integers such as 2, 3, 4, 5, 6, 7, 8, 9, 11, and so on. You also want to check the remainder to see if any of these numbers exactly divide into 61. If you were to find a number other than 1 or 61 that exactly divides into 61, then 61 is not a prime number. This procedure is critical to how the algorithm is going to be written."

In addition to verbally communicating this process to students via the virtual session, Nadia projects a PPT slide that has a specific eight-step process on how to implement the three distinct algorithm components:

1. Start.
2. Choose an integer between 3 and 100 that is to be tested for prime (call it N).
3. Choose an integer that is greater or equal to 2 (≥ 2) and less than N ($<$N) (call it D).
4. Divide N by D.
5. If the remainder is zero, then N is not prime, go to the next N (N − N + 1) and divide by D again.
6. If the remainder is not zero, go to the next D (D = D + 1) or if this is the last D then N is prime.
7. Print "N is prime."
8. Go to the next N (N = N + 1), or if this is the last N, stop.

Nadia then projects another PPT slide that shows a flowchart depicting the same process (see Figure 6.1). For such assignments, it is always useful to sketch a flowchart to demonstrate that an algorithm is finite (has a start and stop) and in this case, the decision and repeat logic (loop logic) are depicted by the diamond-shaped polygons. Nadia also annotates the flowchart to identify which parts of the programming language C are needed to implement the decision and repeat logic. For example, steps 2 and 3 each require a "for loop" in C, steps 5 and 6 are implemented using a decision statement ("if-then-else"), and step 7 requires the print statement (see Figure 6.1).

Next, Nadia models how to convert the algorithm from the flowchart into a computer program using the C programming language projecting related slides. Finally, Nadia projects two related PPT slides. The first consists of the questions related to the monitoring phase and the second

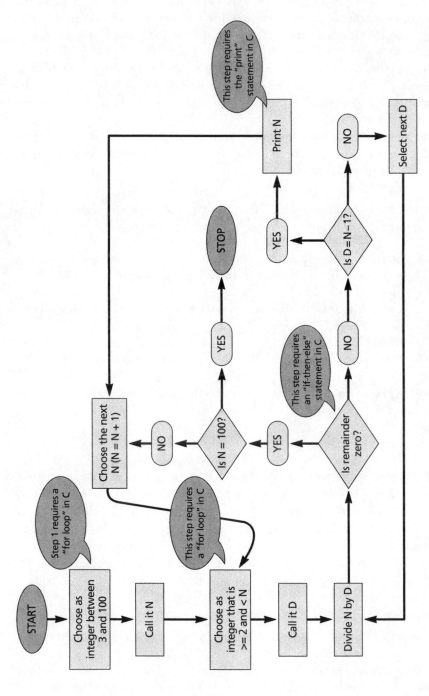

Figure 6.1 Annotated flowchart for computer programming algorithm.

consists of the questions related to the evaluation phase (see Table 6.3). Nadia then uses the questions in the monitoring and evaluation phases as a checklist (Yes/No/Not Sure) and proceeds to answer them accordingly. For those questions that she answers "no" or "not sure," she provides advice on what to do or where to get help. For example, she shows students several resources embedded in the course website as well as other help-seeking features such as the course e-mail feature for contacting the instructor or the teaching assistant (if applicable).

In summary, Nadia uses both verbal (think-aloud) and visual (PPT slides) elements to demonstrate or model for students how she approached this computer programming problem using planning, monitoring, and evaluation processes. The advantages of using a virtual session during the observation phase are that students can ask questions in real time via the chat feature (because it is a live session), and students can access the presentation later and go through it at their own pace (because a virtual session can be archived). Students can also take notes, record information, and write down questions that they can later e-mail to the instructor. Nadia encourages her students to do so several times during the live virtual session.

Once the students have finished observing the problem-solving process from a self-reflective point of view, it is time for them to emulate the process in the instructor's presence (emulation phase) so that the instructor can provide coaching and feedback on their performance. To enable this process, Nadia asks each student to prepare a video using YouTube or a similar video creation tool to demonstrate how they would apply the self-reflective practice checklist to solve a programming example similar to the one she demonstrated in the observation phase. This activity makes students feel empowered, because they are creating their own content using a Web 2.0 tool, a learning exercise that many educators believe is inherently valuable. Nadia asks each student to post the video to the course website in a private area so that only she and the student can view it. This creates a nonthreatening environment that encourages active participation in the learning process. Additionally, it allows the instructor to provide specific feedback on each student's performance using ILT (e.g., collaborative and communication tools). The critical issue in the emulation phase is teaching students like John how to approach solving a problem by breaking it into manageable and achievable tasks (proximal and process goals). Another goal of the emulation phase is to help students like John build confidence and self-efficacy as they gain mastery of the learning process.

Developing a performance-based video is also a great technique for engaging students in self-monitoring. Students can always revisit their video to monitor their learning progress. Moreover, Nadia provides feedback on each student's video to promote accuracy and to encourage students to perform the newly learned skill in the absence of instructor support. Nadia also encourages students to join a professional group on Facebook that specifically addresses issues related to programming in C language. Facebook groups support a learning community model that can foster identity building and confidence, which is what John needs to succeed in this course. This specific learning community can also provide participants with a range of tools to collaborate and share information. Students can share their videos and receive feedback from experts and peers if they choose to do so. As do many college students, John already has an account on Facebook, so he is motivated to join this group.

During the self-control phase, John will begin practicing the learning task on his own. This is a critical step toward helping students become self-regulated learners. To enable this process, Nadia creates small student groups and provides each group with as many homework problems as there are members. The idea is for each student to solve a problem individually (in this case, write an algorithm in step and flowchart formats) and share the problem solution with the group members. She asks each group to assign a member who will take the lead in organizing this process in a collaborative area using Google Docs and Google Calendar to keep track of the group's submissions and progress.

John uses the self-reflective practice checklist to break down the problem into manageable steps and puts a checkmark next to each step as he completes it. As students begin completing their algorithms and posting them to their designated group area, Nadia can provide additional feedback and problem-solving tips using the editing and annotating features of Google Docs. Nadia also asks group members to provide peer feedback on each other's algorithms by converting them into code and testing them to see if they generate the required output. Once John has mastered the problem solving process using self-reflective practice in this phase of the training model, he is ready to progress to the self-regulation phase.

In essence, this phase marks the transition from a focus based on process to one based on outcome. John will need to reflect upon his performance and modify and adapt his behavior based upon self-evaluation as needed. At this level, the primary sources of motivation will be John's intrinsic interest in solving similar tasks on his own and his self-efficacy beliefs to effectively complete programming and design assignments. Nadia feels assured that John can apply the self-reflective practice skills he has learned as he approaches problem-solving tasks in subsequent, advanced courses.

Conclusion

This chapter described how instructors can use ILT to support and promote student self-monitoring and self-evaluation. Specifically, the chapter provided examples of how ILT can be used to help students carefully plan their assignments, keep records of their progress, and use this information to make judgments about their performance. The chapter also described how instructors can use ILT to provide students with ILT to provide students with individual as well as collaborative feedback on how well they are progressing toward the intended goal. Engaging students in self-reflection using ILT can prompt them to approach self-monitoring and self-evaluation with a more adaptive mindset to modify their learning in an effort to improve future performance.

References

Butler, D., & Winne, P. H. (1995). Feedback and self-regulated learning: A theoretical synthesis. *Review of Educational Research, 65,* 245–282.

Dabbagh, N., & Kitsantas, A. (2005). Using web-based pedagogical tools as scaffolds for self-regulated learning. *Instructional Science, 33*(5–6), 513–540.

Dabbagh, N., & Kitsantas, A. (2009). *How do experienced online instructors use Integrative Learning Technologies (ILT) to support student self-regulation and learning?* Unpublished manuscript, George Mason University, Fairfax, VA.

Gynnild, V., Holstad, A., & Myrhaug, D. (2008). Identifying and promoting self-regulated learning in higher education: Roles and responsibilities of student tutors. *Mentoring & Tutoring: Partnership in Learning, 16*(2), 147–161.

Kitsantas, A., & Dabbagh, N. (2004). Promoting self-regulation in distributed learning environments with web-based pedagogical tools: An exploratory study. *Journal on Excellence in College Teaching, 15*(1–2), 119–142.

Kitsantas, A., Zimmerman, B. J. (2006). Enhancing self-regulation of practice: The influence of graphing and self-evaluative standards. *Metacognition and Learning, 3,* 201–212.

Lan, W. (1996). The effects of self-monitoring on students' course performance, use of learning strategies, attitude, self-judgment ability, and knowledge representation. *Journal of Experimental Education, 64,* 101–115.

Pressley, M., & Ghatala, E. S. (1990). Self-regulated learning: Monitoring learning from text. *Educational Psychologist, 25,* 19–33.

Schraw, G. (1998). Promoting general metacognitive awareness. *Instructional Science, 26,* 113–125.

Schunk, D. H., & Ertmer, P. A. (1999). Self-regulatory processes during computer skill acquisition: Goal and self-evaluative influences. *Journal of Educational Psychology, 91,* 251–260.

Schunk, D. H., & Ertmer, P. A. (2000). Self-regulation and academic learning: Self-efficacy enhancing interventions. In M. Boekaerts, P. R. Pintrich, & M. Ziedner (Eds.), *Handbook of self-regulation* (pp. 631–649). San Diego, CA: Academic Press.

Schunk, D. H, Pintrich, P. R., & Meece, J. (2008). *Motivation in education: Theory, research and applications* (3rd ed.). Upper Saddle River, NJ: Pearson Education.

Schunk, D. H., & Zimmerman, B. J. (Eds.). (1998). *Self-regulated learning: From teaching to self-reflective practice.* New York: The Guilford Press.

Vanderbilt, A. A. (2005). Designed for teachers: How to implement self-monitoring in the classroom. *Beyond Behavior, 15*(1), 21-24. Retrieved February 14, 2008 from http://www.ccbd.net/documents/bb/Fall2005vol-15no1pp21-24.pdf

Zimmerman, B. J. (1995). Self-efficacy and educational development. In A. Bandura (Ed.), *Self-efficacy in changing societies* (pp. 202–231). New York: Cambridge University Press.

Zimmerman, B. J. (1999). Commentary: Toward a cyclically interactive view of self-regulated learning. *International Journal of Educational Research, 31,* 545–551.

Zimmerman, B. J. (2000). Attaining self-regulation: A social cognitive perspective. In M. Boekaerts, P. R. Pintrich, & M. Ziedner (Eds.), *Handbook of self-regulation* (pp. 13–39). San Diego, CA: Academic Press.

Zimmerman, B. J. (2008). Investigating self-regulation and motivation: Historical background, methodological developments, and future prospects. *American Educational Research Journal, 45,* 166–183

Zimmerman, B. J., & Kitsantas, A. (2005). The hidden dimension of personal competence: Self-regulated learning and practice. In A. J. Elliot and C. S. Dweck (Eds.), *Handbook of competence and motivation* (pp. 204–222). New York: Guilford Press.

7

Time Management

Contents

Learning to Learn with Integrative Learning Technologies, pages 109–128
Copyright © 2010 by Information Age Publishing

Scenario

> *Time management is like juggling a bunch of tennis balls: for most of us, juggling doesn't come naturally, but it is a skill that can be learned.*
>
> —Robert S. Feldman (2007, p. 30)

David is an instructor of a large math course at a university. Many of David's students are taking this course because it is a general education requirement. The course must be completed with a grade of C or higher in order for students to register in advanced math courses. However, David has many freshmen students who are lacking time-management skills. Many of the students are unaware of how to set goals and organize and structure their environment and time.

Lisa is just one student that exemplifies the problems students are having in David's course. Lisa is a first-semester freshman. During the first few weeks of the fall, Lisa enjoyed her new freedom and the opportunity to meet new friends, frequenting many parties and social events. Although she was an above-average student in high school, Lisa spent very little time studying. Frequently, she delayed preparing for an exam until the night before, when she would spend several hours cramming. Lisa often procrastinated and put off her academic tasks until the last possible minute. This strategy seemed to work for Lisa in high school as she managed to graduate with a good GPA.

Now that Lisa is facing her first series of midterm exams, she realizes that she is not prepared. As she reviews the study guide several days before the math midterm she becomes overwhelmed with the amount of information she must learn for the test. Lisa is discouraged and becomes increasingly anxious as the day of the midterm approaches. Because of her mounting anxiety, she becomes distracted and unable to focus while studying. In her frustration, Lisa decides to go to a party the night before the midterm, since there is no way she can do well, given her lack of preparation. Not surprisingly, Lisa scores 68/100 on the math midterm.

Fortunately, Lisa contacts the instructor immediately after she receives her exam to discuss her performance in the class. After asking Lisa about her study habits, David recognizes that Lisa is having difficulty managing her time effectively. David presents Lisa with several options, such as setting appropriate goals and creating a time frame for accomplishing those goals. Lisa is receptive and incorporates these strategies into her daily schedule. Several weeks later, she reports that she has been able to use these strategies to prepare for her other classes as well. Lisa ends the semester with a B in David's course. More important, Lisa feels better prepared to meet the challenges of more-advanced courses in her degree program.

What Is Time Management?

Time management is characterized as how a student balances and plans his or her time to allow for goal-directed activities (Claessens et al., 2007). As students transition from high school to college, they must be able to balance academic demands. Examples of time-management behaviors include (a) time assessment behaviors that help identify one's time use; (b) planning behaviors such as setting goals, planning tasks, and prioritizing tasks; and (c) monitoring behaviors aimed at observing one's use of time while performing activities to evaluate it (Pintrich, 2004). Therefore, effective time management involves recognizing and visualizing the realization of a goal, identifying potential obstacles and revising original plans to resolve any goal conflict, and finally enacting the plans to achieve the goal (Simons & Galotti, 1992). These aspects of time management are related to academic performance and stress levels (Macan et al., 1990; Oaten & Cheng, 2006).

Research on Time Management: Implications for Instruction

The inability to effectively manage time is a critical issue for many undergraduate students. In order to learn how to manage time effectively, individuals must become aware of, recognize, and acknowledge the ways in which they waste time in order to work more efficiently. For example, some common time wasters include daydreaming, procrastinating, watching TV, playing video games, and talking to friends on the phone, among others (Dembo, 2000). These behaviors may or may not be inherently bad; however, if they occur during the time students should be studying, they become problematic. Learning to recognize the obstacles that preclude effective use of time can be a first step for students toward the development of adaptive behaviors.

Several researchers (e.g., Kiewra & DuBois, 1998; Ruban & Reis, 2006) recommend that students use a checklist to assess their use of time-management behaviors. Other researchers (e.g., Feldman, 2007) suggest that students create a time log to keep track of how they spend their time, and that they fill out evaluation questionnaires that can help them identify their "procrastination quotient" and "time style." Massachusetts Institute of Technology (MIT) provides a "time distribution assessment" (see http://web. mit.edu/uaap/learning/modules/time/assessment.pdf) that allows students to evaluate their time-management methods by documenting how they spend their time in a week, accounting for all 168 hours and using a variety of categories that include academics, jobs, sleep, meals, extracurricular activities, and free time. These instruments and strategies can help students become aware of how effectively they are controlling and managing their time.

Research suggests that students who keep careful records of time spent on assigned learning tasks begin to recognize patterns in their own use of study time and develop an appreciation for the value of effective time management and its impact on academic achievement (Zimmerman, 2000). Effective time management is essential to successful problem solving across different domains because it prompts students to recognize goals and available resources, as well as foresee potential obstacles that may prevent goal achievement (Simons & Galotti, 1992). Once students have identified the specific ways they waste time (or procrastinate) and have assessed their use of time-management strategies, they are in a better position to create and implement new strategies to replace the time wasters. Conversely, students ineffective time-management skills have been associated with stress and poor academic performance (Macan et al., 1990).

Time management has been found to be a consistent predictor of college academic success across the first two academic years of study (Kitsantas, Winsler, & Huie, 2008). Specifically, Kitsantas et al. (2008) surveyed college freshmen on various motivational and self-regulatory variables to predict their achievement two years later. The results suggest that among time management, task value, metacognitive self-regulation, self-efficacy, and prior achievement (e.g., high school GPA and math and verbal SAT scores), time management was the most potent predictor of achievement across the two years of study. This suggests that time-management strategies (a) play an integral part in student achievement above and beyond other motivational and self-regulatory factors, and (b) are important to student achievement not only during the beginning of their studies, but also as they progress through their academic career.

In a related study, Oaten and Cheng (2006) investigated the effects of a self-regulatory intervention on overriding unhealthy and maladaptive impulses (i.e., procrastination, substance use, inability to adhere to study schedules) and stress related to exams. The intervention included the implementation of artificial early deadlines according to students' course requirements. These deadlines required students to break down distant goals into smaller, proximal, specific, and achievable goals. The intervention also helped students to design and implement a study schedule, and provided them with a study diary to promote student self-monitoring and generation of feedback related to their study progress. The results of the study indicated that students who were part of the self-regulatory intervention exhibited significant improvements in self-regulatory capacity relative to the control group. Students exposed to the intervention also showed significant increases in self-control (i.e., improved study habits and healthy eating) and significant decreases in unhealthy behaviors during exams. These findings suggest that self-regulatory interventions designed to effectively plan and monitor study behaviors (in this case, time management) can have a positive effect on academic performance and other lifestyle behaviors.

Time-management practices have also been found to predict SAT scores and subsequent college GPA scores in undergraduate students (Britton & Tesser, 1991). In this study by Britton and Tesser factor analyses indicated that time management consisted of three factors: short-range planning, time attitudes, and long-range planning. Short-range planning included items related to daily or weekly planning, such as making a daily to-do list. Time attitudes were used to describe items, such as feeling in control of how time was spent and using time effectively. Long-range planning included items related to setting goals for the entire quarter and being well organized. The analyses revealed that short-range planning and time attitudes explained 21 percent of the variance in cumulative college GPA scores (after four years), which was higher than the variance explained by SAT scores. Long-range planning did not correlate with GPA in this study sample. Overall, the results of this study revealed evidence to support that time-management behaviors, specifically short-term planning and time attitudes, predict academic performance. Moreover, the strength of these predictors was greater than SAT scores in predicting final GPA. These findings emphasize the need to incorporate short-term goal planning into instruction.

Overall, research suggests that effective time management for students involves a clear understanding of the goal, the ability to break down the larger goal into smaller tasks, appropriate planning, and an accurate appraisal of the time needed to complete the specific tasks to attain the desired goal(s) (Dembo, 2000). Thus, the question is, How can college instructors instill in students a sense of the importance of time management and what specifically can students do to increase their ability to manage their time? Researchers (see Dembo, 2000; Zimmerman, Bonner, & Kovach, 1996) suggest that instructors should emphasize the following skills: (a) setting specific times for study, (b) creating a suitable study environment, (c) chunking tasks into manageable time frames of 30 to 60 minutes, (d) incorporating short breaks, (e) identifying specific plans for use of time, (f) alternating subjects when long periods of time are available for study, (g) estimating the time needed for each task, (h) prioritizing tasks in order of importance, (i) completing less interesting assignments first, (j) planning for assignments in advance, and (k) utilizing a calendar to record events and reviewing the calendar daily.

Correspondingly, MIT suggests ten "simple ways to save time" for students on its Time Management and Organization Online Learning Module (see http://web.mit.edu/uaap/learning/modules/time/savetime.html). These include (1) making the alarm clock your friend; (2) making waiting time productive by using it to complete tasks incrementally, such as continuing with a reading assignment or reviewing lecture notes; (3) breaking large or challenging tasks and assignments into smaller parts or components using a task or assignment timeline; (4) keeping a prioritized daily to-do list; (5) organizing your work space; (6) consuming information selectively; (7) stopping others from stealing your time; (8) using e-mail and instant/text messaging in moderation (try to limit yourself to one hour a day or a half hour in the morning and a half hour in the evening); (9) using technology to make your life easier (e.g., use electronic planners that allow multiple views to calendars and schedules); and (10) OHIO: Only Handle It Once (e.g., go through your print mail or e-mail once by opening it and filing it in the appropriate place).

As depicted in the scenario at the beginning of this chapter, instructors can play a critical role in helping students control and manage their time. The student in the chapter scenario, Lisa, sought the help of her instructor, David, after receiving a low score on the math midterm and he was able to suggest strategies to help her manage her time. However, most students will not seek the instructor's help; rather, they will give themselves excuses to fail or drop out of college. Instructors can have a positive effect on their students if they integrate time-management strategies in their courses and if they model effective time-management techniques for their students. For example, Zimmerman et al. (1996) suggest that instructors create a three-phase (planning, implementation, and follow-up) time-management guide to help students effectively manage course assignment completion. Specifically, in the planning phase, instructors can design assignments that are comparable in terms of length and difficulty and align them with time-management activities. In the implementation phase, instructors can collect baseline time-management data about their students and incorporate time-management activities as well as provide forms to help students monitor completion of daily assignments. For example, a form can include columns to record the date, the assignment, the time the assignment was started, how long it took to complete the assignment, the environment in which the assignment was completed, and a column for the student to record their self-efficacy rating. Instructors can then compare these ratings with students' actual grades on assignments. The process of engaging students in predicting their expected score or grade on an assignment or test, and their self-efficacy belief to attain this score, will reveal any discrepancies in a student's self-efficacy beliefs and actual performance, whether accurate, high, or low, which can then be addressed.

In the follow-up phase, instructors can create follow-up activities later in the semester to assess student time-management skill development over time.

Instructors can also help their students create calendars and semester plans to facilitate time management. For example, they can ask students to bring the course syllabus, personal calendars, planning agendas, PDAs, and other mobile electronic devices regularly to class and can schedule class time for students to use them for time-management purposes. Instructors can help students identify or predict the busiest weeks of their first semester in college and then have students think about how they plan to use this information to make the best use of their time. Students may need assistance moving between daily or weekly calendars and semester plans, and instructors can help them discriminate small steps or tasks that should be completed daily or weekly to ensure the successful completion of major assignments, projects, and tests (Feldman, 2007). Instructors can also design activities around time management by having students share or exchange their semester calendars with other students and provide suggestions to one another for improving time use. Instructors can also assure students that understanding the process of planning and managing time can help them balance their personal, professional, and academic lives so they can become successful students. As Feldman (2007) posits:

> The goal of time management is not to schedule every moment so we become pawns of a timetable that governs every waking moment of the day. Instead the goal is to permit us to make informed choices as to how we use our time. (p. 31)

In traditional, face-to-face classroom settings, the instructor exercises significant control over the learning process and is able to monitor student attention and progress closely (Besser & Bonn, 1997). Hence, it is easier to create, implement, and monitor a time-management system in this kind of setting. However, in online or distributed learning environments, time management becomes very critical because students must be highly self-regulated in order to accomplish their learning goals (Dabbagh & Kitsantas, 2004). Therefore, instructors must be ready to utilize Integrative Learning Technologies (ILT) to develop a time-management system that supports and promotes effective time-management skills in students so that they can successfully complete the course requirements.

Supporting and Promoting Time Management Using ILT

Overall, three ILT categories—collaborative and communication tools, content creation and delivery tools, and learning tools—were found to be particularly useful in assisting students with time-management strategies in online or distributed learning environments (Dabbagh & Kitsantas, 2005; Kitsantas & Dabbagh, 2004). For example, when instructors used the course syllabus feature of an LMS (a content creation and delivery tool) to post the weekly, monthly, and semester timeline, students were encouraged to plan their course work effectively. Additionally, the personal electronic calendar (a learning tool) was found to be very useful in helping students to effectively plan and manage their semester activities. Also, when instructors posted specific protocols and rubrics that informed students how to engage in an online discussion (see http://mason.gmu.edu/~ndabbagh/wblg/online-protocol.html), students were able to effectively budget their time and successfully contribute to the discussion forum. These findings suggest that ILT can be very effective in helping students learn time-management strategies. In fact, Loomis (2000) found that students' ability to effectively manage time in online or distributed learning environments is a predictor of their ability to succeed.

In a recent survey conducted by Dabbagh and Kitsantas (2009), instructors proficient in using ILT to design, develop, and deliver their college courses were asked how they used ILT to help their students with time management. The results of the survey revealed that the online calendar and syllabus tools were most effective in communicating to students the course schedule, timelines, and assignment due dates. Table 7.1 provides a snapshot of how these instructors utilized ILT tools to model effective time management.

Additionally researchers have recommended that specific guidelines should be followed when designing ILT tools to support effective time management. More specifically, Terry and Doolittle (2006) recommended

TABLE 7.1   Instructors' Use of ILT to Support Time Management

Time management strategy	Example of ILT use to support time management
Helping your students effectively plan and manage their time	• "I use the syllabus to post the course timeline and the last slide of each presentation to explain and remind students what is due for the following week." • "I use the Blackboard LMS to upload PowerPoint files and discussion questions before class to help students effectively budget their time while studying and post the syllabus, which contains upcoming assignments." • "The CMS (Moodle) assigns dates to the activities and assignments, so the students can look up the dates in Moodle's internal calendar system." • "I use WebCT's calendar tool to post the weekly class schedule and identify due dates." • "I use WebCT's syllabus feature to post a schedule prepared in Word."

the use of five strategies that instructors can use to promote student time-management skills in distributed learning environments: (1) clearly communicate deadlines and due dates, (2) encourage goal setting, (3) provide checklists and organizers, (4) provide feedback, and (5) scaffold regular check-in processes. Table 7.2 illustrates how ILT categories and tools can be used to support these strategies in an online course.

Additional techniques of using technology to improve time-management skills were described by Bennett (2007) who writes the technology column for The Sydney Morning Herald (see http://www.smh.com.au/news/home-office/ten-ways-to-improve-time-management/2007/04/29/1177787955900.html). These techniques ranged from using e-mail software such as Microsoft Outlook to display your task list on your desktop and program e-mail reminders, to using web-based tools such as HiTask (www.hitask.com), Todoist (todoist.com), and Google Calendar to create and store to-do lists, projects, and calendars on the web, so you can access them anywhere, anytime and share them with colleagues to coordinate schedules and meetings. Bennett also suggests using the Notepad application or Microsoft Word to create simple text files to save and print your to-do lists. Mobile technologies like your cell phone, PDA, or even an iPod can be used to download text-based to-do lists, schedules, and calendars. These portable technologies can be carried in your pocket and may be more convenient than trying to log onto the Internet to access your time organizers. Instructors can model the use

TABLE 7.2   Developing a Time-Management System Using ILT

Time-management strategy	ILT categories and tools
Clearly communicate course deadlines and due dates	• Instructors can use the online calendar of an LMS (an administrative tool) and calendar sharing tools (e.g., Google Calendar) to provide a timeline of events, activities, and required course outputs • Instructors can coach students to use the personal calendar, personal tasks features of an LMS (learning tools), or a PDA (personal digital assistant) to set their own work/study timetables • Instructors can use the course management features of an LMS (administrative tools) to selectively release assignments, assessments, and course announcements based on specific dates or preselected criteria (e.g., grade) and to link course activities to specific dates or course events
Encourage goal setting	• Instructors can use the content module or learning units features of an LMS (content creation and delivery tools) to break down the course and assignments into modules that have specific beginning and end dates to encourage students to set proximal, attainable, and time dependent goals • Instructors can use collaborative and communication tools to develop (using a word processer) a time-dependent goals checklist associated with each learning module and e-mail it to students to encourage goal-setting behavior
Provide checklists and organizers	• Instructors can use the assignment feature of an LMS (a content creation and delivery tool) to develop time-dependent or calendar-style checklists for each assignment, course task, or course activity • Instructors can use course planning and scheduling tools of an LMS (administrative tools) to provide a bird's-eye view of course components and events • Instructors can use content creation and delivery tools to develop to-do lists, checklists, or rubrics that include content- and strategy-related information to promote self-monitoring of time management based on lists of tasks and organizers

Time-management strategy	ILT categories and tools
Provide feedback	• Instructors can use asynchronous tools (e.g., e-mail or discussion forums) and synchronous tools (e.g., chat and virtual sessions) to provide feedback to students on their performance on assignments and course activities • Instructors can provide contextualized feedback using the comments feature of weblogs and wikis when students are asked to develop their assignments and group projects using these tools • Instructors can use assessment tools to design quizzes, tests, or self-assessment rubrics that provide automated feedback
Scaffold regular check-in processes	• Instructors can use student tracking tools (administrative tools) to track the frequency and duration of student access to course components in order to monitor their learning progress • Instructors can encourage students to use learning tools that report modules accessed and time spent on course components to help them determine whether they have spent sufficient time on materials and whether they have missed anything

of these technologies to their students and encourage them to use them effectively to plan and manage their time and academic tasks.

Overall, instructors should use ILT to develop and model time-management activities that support and promote students' planning behaviors such as setting goals, planning tasks, prioritizing, making to-do lists, and grouping tasks; time-assessment behaviors, which aim at awareness of one's time use; and monitoring behaviors, which aim at observing one's use of time while performing activities (Claessens et al., 2007).

Training Students for Effective Time Management

We will now apply the four-phased self-regulation training model described in Chapters 1 and 3 to demonstrate how David, the instructor in the scenario at the beginning of this chapter, can help his students, in this case Lisa, acquire effective time-management skills to become successful academically. In the observation phase, David needs to model to students effective time-management strategies. David can begin by using a Learning Management System (LMS) to organize the course content, particularly the course timeline. LMS have embedded calendars (an administrative tool) that instructors can use to generate semester timelines (see Figure 7.1).

Advantages of using an LMS calendar include the ability to see multiple views of the calendar or course timeline by clicking on a specific week or day. David should take time in class or online via a virtual session (a collaborative and communication tool) to demonstrate to students how he developed the LMS calendar and how it can be used. He can also demonstrate how students can add their own notes to this calendar and create their own personal schedule using this calendar as a starting point (student entries will remain private); or he can recommend using other tools such as Google Calendar. David can also embed the semester timeline in the syllabus as a table that depicts the major assignments and exams with due dates. Many students print out the syllabus, so it is important to have the timeline embedded in the syllabus document. By doing this, David is modeling different techniques of generating a master schedule or semester timeline using ILT. David can also use the LMS course planning and scheduling tools (see administrative tools in Chapter 2) to create a menu of course components (see the sidebar in Figure 7.1), using meaningful labels to make the course components and resources more relevant to students as well as easy to find.

Next David can model how to create an assignment task list and timeline to demonstrate to students how to break down an assignment into smaller and manageable subtasks. Given that he is teaching a required general education math class, David knows that all his students need to get a minimum grade of C in order to pass this class; therefore, preparing for the midterm is a very important task that requires effective time management. David decides to develop a webcast to demonstrate to his students how to plan for the midterm. An advantage of using a webcast is that it can be linked to the course website so that students can access it anytime, anywhere and use it as a model to plan for other assignments. David can also use this webcast in future courses. During the recording of this webcast, he emphasizes to his students that in order to do well in his or any other class, they need to plan ahead and pace themselves instead of cramming for the test at the last minute, because cramming is not conducive to deep learning. David also emphasizes to his students that planning ahead will help them gauge the amount of effort they need to put into preparing for this task relative to other academic tasks and obligations due in the same time frame. He reminds students that they should include all academic tasks and due dates from all their course work on the master or semester calendar that they will create.

Then David proceeds to generate a five-column table (see Table 7.3) using Microsoft Word to model effective time management for preparing

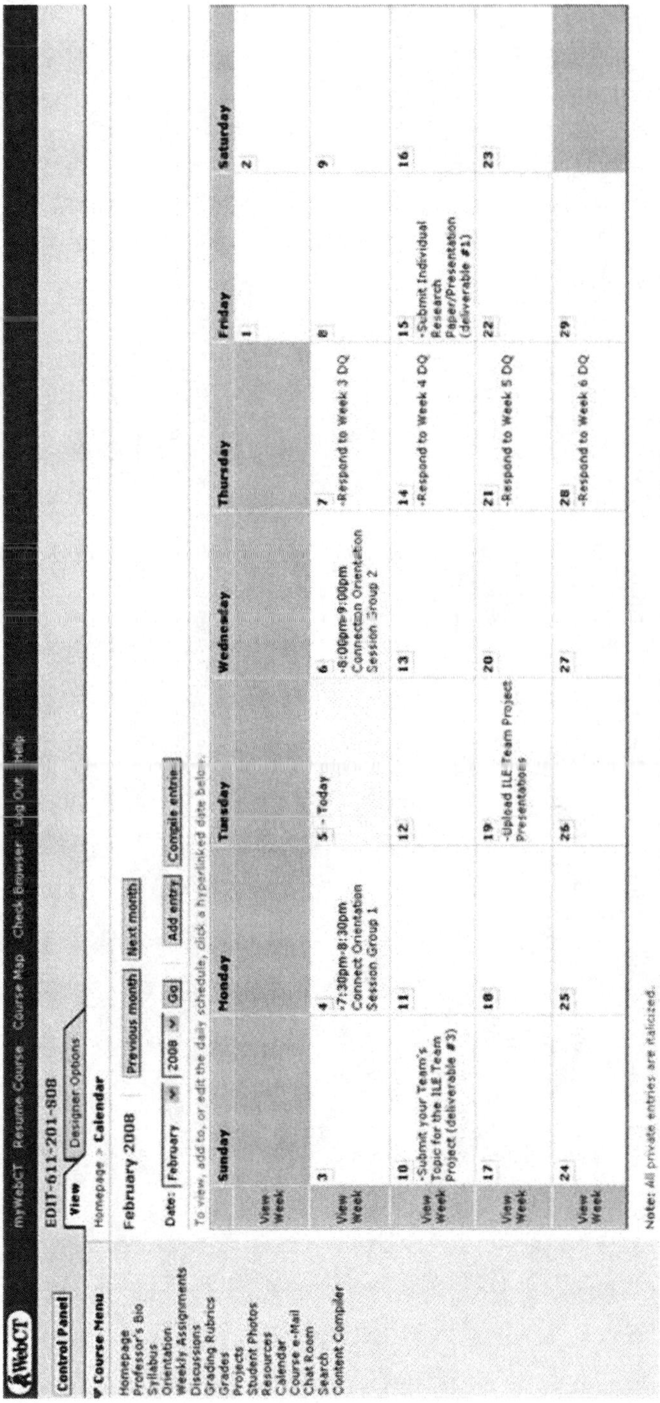

Figure 7.1 An example of an instructor-created course calendar using an LMS.

TABLE 7.3 Training Students for Setting Time-Management Strategies

Midterm planning	Questions to ask yourself	Where and how to get answers	How much time will this take?	Checkmark column
Exam logistics	• What is the date and time of the exam? • Where is the exam? • How long will I have to take the exam? • Can I bring a calculator or formula sheet? • Will the test be open book/notebook? • What will the format of the test be? (e.g., multiple-choice, short answer, or problems) • What percentage of the final grade is this exam worth?	• Check the course syllabus or website • Check the course calendar or timeline • E-mail the instructor if you cannot find the information in the course documentation. • Write down your answers in your notebook or on your calendar	• This could be answered in minutes depending where the information related to exam logistics is located	Place a checkmark in this column across from each question listed in the second column once you have answered the question or completed a related task
Exam content	• Does the instructor expect you to have mastered the material covered between certain dates or within certain chapters of your text? • Will information in handouts and other supplemental materials be covered on the exam?	• Check the course syllabus or website • Check your lecture or course notes • Check course handouts. • Check your e-mail or the LMS/course e-mail to see if there are specific e-mails from your instructor regarding the test	• This could take minutes or it could take a couple of hours, depending on how easily and quickly you are able to find this information	

- Is the exam cumulative? Is there any overlap between material covered on this test and that covered on previous exams?
- Does success on this exam depend on mastery of concepts that have eluded you on prior tests?
- Is the instructor currently teaching material that will not be covered on the upcoming test, but will likely be on the following one?

- E-mail the instructor if you cannot find the information in the course documentation
- Ask the instructor
- Sift through all your course materials

Study plan

- How much time do I have to prepare for the exam?
- How many chapters do I have to study or review?
- Are there any handouts that I need to study or review?
- How much lecture notes do I have to go over?
- Are there homework assignments that I need to review?
- What other exams or obligations do I have the week of the exam?
- How confident do I feel about the exam content?
- Will I study alone, with a friend, or in a study group?

- Make a schedule of your free time each day between now and exam time.
- Spread your study time across these free times
- Use shorter free time blocks to review lecture notes or practice problems
- Prepare a study checklist that sequences or prioritizes what you will focus on (e.g., chapters, study notes, and practice problems)
- Identify content problem areas and schedule times to meet with the instructor

- This could take between 2–10 hours depending on study habits, material to be reviewed, and knowledge of content for a midterm. In the first column, he types (and verbally articulates) three midterm-taking tasks that students should take into consideration while preparing: exam logistics, exam content, and exam preparation or study plan. In the second column, he types (and verbally articulates) task-related questions that students need to ask themselves. In the third column, he types (and verbally articulates) resources and techniques that students can use to get answers to questions listed in the second column. Then he estimates the average time required to complete each task and types this into the fourth column (while verbally articulating how he arrived at these time estimates). He also adds a fifth checkmark column, instructing students to use this column to check off tasks as they complete them.

In the emulation phase of the training model, students are now ready to emulate the time-management strategies that David has demonstrated. David asks his students to create, as a course assignment, their own personal master semester calendar using the LMS student calendar option or Google Calendar and to upload their calendars to the course website for instructor and peer feedback. David also asks each student to develop a table similar to the table he used in the observation phase to articulate their study plan for the first midterm in his class. By developing such a table, students are using the personal tasks feature of learning tools (see chapter 2) to increase their autonomy and self-directed learning capacity by setting their own work/study timetables in support of learning outcomes. David also asks the students to upload their study plans to the course website for instructor feedback. To help students prepare the master calendar and task table, David asks students to evaluate their time-management skills by taking a variety of inventories and self-tests that he makes available on the course website.

In phase 3 of the training model, the self-control phase, students are supposed to focus on mastering the processes related to completing the learning task during practice episodes. In this case, the learning task is to learn how master any course related task by using effective time-management strategies. To provide practice, David asks students to go on a "treasure hunt" through his course content and document the following in a master schedule using appropriate columns and labels: How many assignments are there in this course? What is the percentage grade on each assignment? When is each assignment due? What format is it due in? Are there group projects in this course? If so, when are these due and how are the students graded? How many exams are there in this course? What are the dates of these exams? What percentage of the grade is each exam worth? What is the format of each exam? Are there any quizzes in this course? Are they pop quizzes or planned quizzes? If planned, what are the dates of these

Course Introduction Quiz

This activity is designed to test your ability to find information on the course web site. I have found that familiarizing yourself with the Web site prior to using the site for the course makes the on-line experience more pleasant, mainly because you are not always hunting for things on the site! You should first answer the following questions before accessing the actual quiz on the Course Web Site.

Important
The quiz is located in "Assignments". If you have trouble accessing the quiz on the course web site, be sure to get in touch with me, jmooreu@gmu.edu, and we will work on fixing the problem.

1. What are the required entry skills (i.e., will not be taught) for this course?
2. What are the two sections of the Course Web site that you should check at the beginning of each week?
3. What are the minimum number of hours expected per week for class activities?
4. Where are the "Learning Aids" located on the web site?
5. What is the minimum point percentage necessary for an "A" in this course?
6. In the Class Discussion Forum, you should respond to a posting by: 1) beginning a new thread, 2) posting a short "I agree" message if you agree, 3) providing substantial comments expressed in a concise and succinct manner 4) or providing "flaming" and/or personal comments to classmates.
7. When are the Internet office hours for the Facilitator?
8. What is the penalty for assignments that are submitted after the due date?
9. The total course points for both Instructional Design Modules are 20. (True or False)
10. The period for participating on the Class Discussion Forum is Monday - Sunday. (True or False)
11. There are nine required discussion board participations. (True or False)
12. All assignments, except for discussion board participation, are due on Mondays by 11:59pm. (True or False)
13. The course schedule represents the permanent plan for the course. (True or False)
14. The Team Participation Peer Evaluation will be used to calculate individual course points. (True or False)
15. The Analysis Summary is due March 6. (True or False)
16. The Final Exam is due May 8. (True or False)
17. The Instructional Design Portfolio can be submitted as a PDF document. (True or False)
18. The Implementation Plan is a section in the Instructional Design Portfolio. (True or False)
19. The guidelines and rubrics for the assignments are located in Resources. (True or False)
20. The instructional materials created for the Instructional Design Portfolio must be evaluated by a minimum of 3 target learners. (True or False)

Congratulations! You have completed the activity!
You are now ready to begin working in the course on-line!

Figure 7.2 An example of an instructor-created treasure hunt activity.

quizzes and what percentage of the overall course grade do they represent? What is the total number of points that you can get in this course? What is the corresponding letter grade? What is the passing grade in this course? These questions are designed to encourage students to thoroughly examine their course syllabi and course websites in order to develop effective time-management skills. A sample illustration of a treasure hunt activity titled Course Introduction Quiz is provided in Figure 7.2. These activities and other similar ones allow students to practice task strategies that facilitate time management without direct coaching, as should be the case in the self-control phase of the training model.

In phase 4 of the model, self-regulation, students need to focus on outcomes and make strategic adjustments when performing poorly. With respect to time management, David asks students to evaluate how they did on the first midterm in his class and to reflect on whether the time-management tools and strategies that they used to prepare their calendars, timelines, and study plans had an impact on their performance and whether they would change anything based on their performance. He requires that each student write a reflective blog (a content creation and delivery tool) about this and post any questions that they have on the course discussion forum (a collaborative and communication tool). Lisa reports that these strategies have been effective in helping her not only to prepare for the midterm in this course and do well on it but also in helping her feel better prepared to meet the challenges of more advanced courses in her degree program.

Conclusion

This chapter described how students can be trained to effectively manage their time. Several research studies on time management were reviewed in terms of helping students take control of their time, prioritize their tasks, and manage their time to become successful learners. The chapter also provided examples of how instructors can use ILT to support and promote time-management skills in students in order to optimize their learning.

References

Bennett, B. (2007, April 30). Ten ways to improve time management. *The Sydney Morning Herald*. Retrieved May 12, 2008 from: http://www.smh.com.au/news/home-office/ten-ways-to-improve-time-management/2007/04/29/1177787955900.html

Besser, H., & Bonn, M. (1997). Interactive distance-independent education: Challenges to traditional academic roles. *Journal of Education for Library and Information Science, 38*(1), 35–42.

Britton, B. K., & Tesser, A. (1991). Effects of time management strategies on college grades. *Journal of Educational Psychology, 83*(3), 405–410.

Claessens, B. J. C., van Eerde, W., Rutte, C. G., & Roe, R. A. (2007). A review of the time management literature. *Personnel Review, 36*(2), 255–276.

Dabbagh, N., & Kitsantas, A. (2004). Supporting self-regulation in student-centered web-based learning environments. *International Journal on E- Learning, 3*(1), 40–47.

Dabbagh, N., & Kitsantas, A. (2005). Using web-based pedagogical tools as scaffolds for self-regulated learning. *Instructional Science, 33*(5–6), 513–540.

Dabbagh, N., & Kitsantas, A. (2009). *How do experienced online instructors use Integrative Learning Technologies (ILT) to support student self-regulation and learning?* Unpublished manuscript, George Mason University, Fairfax, VA.

Dembo, M. H. (2000). *Motivation and learning strategies for college success: A self-management approach.* Mahwah, NJ: Lawrence Erlbaum Associates.

Feldman, R. S. (2007). *POWER learning: Strategies for success in college and life* (4th ed.). New York: McGraw-Hill.

Kiewra, K. A., & DuBois, N. F. (1998). *Learning to learn: Making the transition from student to life-long learner.* Boston: Allyn & Bacon.

Kitsantas, A., & Dabbagh, N. (2004). Supporting self-regulation in distributed learning environments with web-based pedagogical tools: An exploratory study. *Journal on Excellence in College Teaching, 15*(1–2), 119–142.

Kitsantas, A., Winsler, A., & Huie, F. (2008). Self-regulation and ability predictors of academic success during college: A predictive validity study. *Journal of Advanced Academics, 20*(1), 42–68.

Loomis, K. D. (2000). Learning styles and asynchronous learning: Comparing the LASSI model to class performance. *Journal of Asynchronous Learning Networks, 4*(1), 23–32.

Macan, T. H., Shahani, C., Dipboye, R. L., & Phillips, A. P. (1990). College students' time management: Correlations with academic performance and stress. *Journal of Educational Psychology, 82,* 760–768.

Massachusetts Institute of Technology. (n.d.). *Time management and organization: Simple ways to save time.* Retrieved September 15, 2008 from: http://web.mit.edu/uaap/learning/modules/time/savetime.html

Oaten, M., & Cheng, K. (2006). Improved self-control: The benefits of a regular program of academic study. *Basic and Applied Social Psychology, 28,* 1–16.

Pintrich, P. R. (2004). A conceptual framework for assessing motivation and self-regulated learning in college students. *Educational Psychology Review, 16,* 385–407.

Ruban, L., & Reis, S. M. (2006). Patterns of self-regulatory strategy use among low-achieving and high-achieving university students. *Roeper Review, 28,* 148–156.

Simons, D. J., & Galotti, K. M. (1992). Everyday planning: An analysis of time management. *Bulletin of the Psychonomic Society, 30,* 61–64.

Terry, K.P., & Doolittle, P. (2006). Fostering self-regulation in distributed learning. *College Quarterly, 9*(1). Retrieved July 13th, 2008 from: http://www.senecac.on.ca/quarterly/2006-vol09-num01-winter/terry_doolittle.html

Zimmerman, B. J. (2000). Attaining self-regulation: A social cognitive perspective. In M. Boekaerts, P. R. Pintrich, & M. Zeidner (Eds.), *Handbook of self-regulation* (pp. 13–39). San Diego: Academic Press.

Zimmerman, B. J., Bonner, S., & Kovach, R. (1996). *Developing self-regulated learners: Beyond achievement to self-efficacy*. Washington, DC: American Psychological Association.

8

Help Seeking

Contents

Learning to Learn with Integrative Learning Technologies, pages 129–142
Copyright © 2010 by Information Age Publishing
All rights of reproduction in any form reserved.

Scenario

My only advice is to stay aware, listen carefully and yell for help if you need it.

—Judy Blume

Cassandra teaches a large undergraduate general chemistry lecture course with an enrollment of about 200 students per semester. Cassandra is constantly looking for ways to make the class more engaging, using technologies such as Clickers, a wireless response system that allows students to respond individually to multiple-choice questions displayed on a large screen and instantaneously view the aggregated class results on a bar graph. A portable computer receiving station placed in the front of the class collects student responses electronically. Cassandra uses Clickers often to gauge student understanding of key chemistry concepts that students must master in order to do well in the course. She also uses Clickers to test for common misconceptions and subsequently discuss these misconceptions with the students. Despite the use of Clickers and other instructional technologies, Cassandra's biggest problem is encouraging students to ask questions in class and attend office hours and study sessions designed to help students understand difficult concepts that will be tested on the exam.

Cassandra understands that many of her students are reluctant to ask instructors for help, particularly in large classes, for fear of being singled out as the only student who does not understand the material. She also remembers from her college days that many students are reluctant to ask their friends content-related questions for fear of feeling embarrassed of portraying themselves as incompetent. Cassandra is determined to find both pedagogical and technological methods that motivate students to seek help when they encounter difficult concepts in their courses or even for clarification purposes. She strongly believes that teaching students how and when to seek help can greatly impact academic success in college and beyond. She decides to conduct more research on help seeking and how it can be supported and implemented in large lecture classes like hers.

What Is Help Seeking?

Help seeking is generally an adaptive self-regulatory process that students utilize when dealing with complex tasks that they either have difficulty completing or feel unable to comprehend on their own (Butler & Winne, 1995; Ryan & Pintrich, 1997). Adaptive help seeking is a goal-directed and intentional behavior that helps academically struggling students achieve their desired goal. Students who engage in adaptive help seeking (a) recognize the need for assistance, (b) identify an appropriate resource, (c) have the motivation and willingness to seek the necessary assistance, and (d) have the determination to employ the strategy to achieve the goal (Karabenick & Knapp, 1991). By contrast, students who engage in nonadaptive help seeking do not know why they need help, have performance or avoidance goal orientations, have a low sense of self-efficacy, and view help seeking as a negative behavior that reveals incompetence (Newman, 2008).

Adaptive and nonadaptive help seeking can be further distinguished based on two main processes, namely (a) self-reflection and (b) affect and motivation (Newman, 2008). Before soliciting help, adaptive help-seeking students, in contrast to nonadaptive help seeking students, self-reflect on how necessary it is to request help (I have tried my best to understand this content on my own, but I am still confused), what specific help they need (What do I need help on? What aspects do I not understand?), and the target of the request (Who would best be able to answer my questions?). In terms of affect and motivation, students who engage in adaptive help-seeking techniques generally set mastery- rather than performance-oriented goals; are self-efficacious about their abilities; and have positive emotions which enable them to share openly with others their areas of weakness in order to strengthen them.

An important aspect of help seeking is the sources of help that students solicit. Potential sources of help can be social or nonsocial in nature and can include instructor support, peer support, and library or Internet resources. Knapp and Karabenick (1988) identified five categories related to seeking help that students use when they are struggling academically. The first two categories are social sources and involve seeking informal assistance from peers and friends and formal assistance from instructors. The last three categories are non-social sources and include activities such as enhanced studying behaviors or more-comprehensive note taking to assist the student to better accomplish the task; lowering performance aspirations or achievement goals such as reducing course load or selecting less demanding course work; and altering goals which can be changing one's school or major.

In summary, the tendency to seek help in response to academic difficulty is related to several factors including (a) recognition of the need for help by the student, (b) willingness of the student to seek help, (c) student's ability to communicate the need to receive the appropriate assistance, and (d) identification of potential resources and strategies. Within this context, help seeking is an adaptive process toward goal achievement on the part of the learner. Hence it is possible to teach students effective help seeking skills.

Research on Help Seeking: Implications for Instruction

Numerous research studies have revealed that many students who need help do not seek assistance because of fears related to self-esteem, which has also been labeled as perceived threat (Karabenick & Knapp, 1991; Newman & Goldin, 1990). In a series of studies, Karabenick (2001), and Karabenick and Knapp (1991) examined correlates of help-seeking behaviors in college students. Findings showed that students are more likely to engage in help-seeking activities when the perceived threat is low. Additionally, students whose help-seeking orientations were more adaptive reported higher levels of motivation (e.g., self-efficacy, intrinsic motivation, mastery goal-orientation), self-regulation (e.g., use of cognitive strategies), and also academically outperformed the students who were more nonadaptive help seekers. Similarly, Ryan and Pintrich (1997) reported that students who perceived themselves as socially competent were more likely to seek help and felt less threatened to engage in help-seeking behavior. On the other hand, students who exhibited feelings of inadequacy related to previous failures were more reluctant to seek help because that could confirm their lack of ability.

With respect to promoting help seeking in a classroom environment, Karabenick and Knapp (1991) concluded that instructors can promote the use of help-seeking activities that can enhance performance when needed. Aspects of the classroom environment that are conducive to help seeking and are generally perceived to be less threatening are characterized by a student-centered approach and a collaborative learning focus. In contrast, instructor emphasis on social comparisons and ego-driven instructional methods creates high-threat environments in which help-seeking behaviors are thwarted.

Many types of help-seeking support have been identified to facilitate adaptive help seeking by students. These include (a) emotional, in which assistance is provided in terms of affective behaviors such as trust and listening; (b) appraisal, in which support is given in the form of positive feed-back; (c) instrumental, in which support is provided in the form of tangible resources such as money or time; and (d) informational, in which support is provided in terms of teaching or advice from formal sources such as an instructor or support services provided by a school, or from informal sources such as friends or peers (Karabenick & Knapp, 1998). See Table 8.1 for specific examples of how these four types of help-seeking support can be implemented in a learning environment using Integrative Learning Technologies (ILT).

Although all types of support are important for student achievement and help-seeking behavior, the patterns of student performance differ according to the type of task assigned and support provided (Tardy, 1992). For example, Tardy found that students who were provided instrumental support on an anagram task improved their performance to a greater degree than students who were given emotional support. In addition, research suggests that certain types of social support are more valuable in certain situations and not all types of support have the same effect on behavior or outcome. Smith and Ragan (1999) recommend that instructors conduct a learner analysis to identify learner characteristics and individual differences, such as, prior knowledge, personality variables, aptitude variables, and cognitive styles that may impact learning and consequently the type of support needed. For example, when learners have high prior knowledge, possess a wide range of cognitive strategies, are flexible and highly motivated, have low anxiety, and attribute success and failure on tasks to internal factors, then instrumental and informational types of help-seeking support are recommended. Alternatively, when learners have low prior knowledge, possess few cognitive strategies, have high anxiety and low motivation, and attribute success and failure to external factors, then emotional and appraisal types of help-seeking support are recommended.

Additionally, the type of help-seeking support provided in a learning environment is highly correlated with the pedagogical approach implemented (Dabbagh, 2003). For example, when a more constructivist or learner-centered pedagogical approach is used, the learning task is generally ill defined and there is high emphasis on critical thinking and collaboration, thus instrumental and informational help-seeking support, particularly informal informational support, should be emphasized. Alternatively, when a more objectivist or instructor-driven pedagogical approach is used, the learning task is generally well defined and there is high emphasis on individual performance and mastery, thus emotional and appraisal types of help-seeking support should be emphasized (Smith & Ragan, 1999).

TABLE 8.1   Types of Help-Seeking Support and ILT Examples

Types of help-seeking	Example of ILT use
Emotional support • Establish a caring atmosphere in which students feel trust, empathy, and encouragement • Establish an open and friendly community of learners	• Ask students to post a short bio to the main discussion forum area of the course to introduce themselves to the class • Use e-mail to encourage and show concern and care for the students. • Ask students to discuss any concerns about course requirements in the main discussion forum area and respond to their concerns • Encourage students to use the chat, discussion, and whiteboard features to discuss and share their ideas with peers
Appraisal support • Provide positive and constructive evaluative feedback on student assignments	• Provide positive feedback on student progress through the e-mail tool • Encourage students to upload rough drafts and work-in-progress to the classwork area of the course, or to attach documents using e-mail, and provide timely feedback
Instrumental support • Provide students with access to resources such as technology support and assistance	• Encourage students to use online dictionaries, electronic libraries, and databases • Provide students with access to online learning materials using the LMS resources tool • Embed a search tool in the LMS to help students find supporting information • Provide an index or a glossary to important terms and concepts
Informational support (both formal and informal) • Provide students with mentoring and coaching • Provide procedural guidance and advice on how to complete tasks • Promote interaction and collaboration • Prompt students to brainstorm different solutions	• Provide one-on-one mentoring and guidance using the e-mail tool • Provide group coaching and facilitation of group tasks and activities using the discussion forum or chat areas • Provide students with tips and cues through the LMS student tips tool • Ask students to provide peer feedback on drafts and work-in-progress • State on your syllabus that students can interact on a one-to-one or one-to-many basis with peers or the instructor using the chat, e-mail, and discussion tools

Overall, extensive research on help seeking has been conducted in classroom environments and there is ample evidence that students who practice adaptive help seeking and demonstrate instrumental and formal styles of help-seeking behavior have better learning outcomes than students who perceive help seeking as a threat (Karabenick, 2001). Although help seeking has been studied to a lesser degree in technology-supported learning environments, a few empirical studies provide encouraging evidence of the potential effectiveness of ILT in supporting help-seeking (Aleven et al., 2004; Aleven et al., 2003; Kitsantas & Chow, 2007). We discuss this research in the next section.

Supporting and Promoting Help Seeking Using ILT

Online environments differ from traditional classroom settings in several distinct and relatively obvious ways. For example, traditional classrooms have the advantage of numerous opportunities for instructors to initiate and maintain supportive interpersonal relationships with students. In contrast, online learning contexts provide few, if any, opportunities for one-on-one student and faculty interaction. Although at first glance this aspect of online learning would seem to preclude students' seeking needed help from the instructor, there is evidence to suggest that the opposite is true. For example, previous research that has examined help-seeking behaviors in college students in a variety of instructional contexts including traditional and distance learning environments has revealed that based upon student self-reports, undergraduates prefer seeking help electronically (e.g., using e-mail, synchronous chat, and discussion boards) (Kitsantas & Chow, 2007). The reasons for this preference appear to be linked to students' feeling more self-efficacious and less threatened when seeking help electronically rather than face-to-face (Kitsantas & Chow, 2007). This suggests that the relative anonymity of online learning could serve to create a low-threat environment for students who tend to be reluctant to ask for assistance (e.g., students with low self-esteem, low social competence, or low-achievement) (see Ryan, Pintrich, & Midgley, 2001). However, it is vital that the instructor provide explicit opportunities for students to seek help, irrespective of the delivery approach of the learning environment, since students are more likely to seek assistance from the instructor when these opportunities are clearly stated (Perrine, Lisle, & Tucker, 1995).

For example, Perrine et al. (1995) investigated students' willingness to seek help from college instructors in relation to student age, student gender, class size, and the effectiveness of a supportive statement included on a course syllabus offering student assistance, if needed. The results of the study indicated that students reported a greater willingness to seek instructor help when a supportive statement was included on the syllabus. The study also revealed that younger students (< 25) were significantly less likely than older students to seek instructor help when a supportive statement was not included on the syllabus. Yet, the willingness to seek help did not differ between younger and older students when instructor support was explicitly stated.

Relatively few studies have investigated help-seeking behaviors in interactive and hypermedia learning environments (Aleven et al., 2003). Godbole-Chaudhuri et al., (2006) evaluated help seeking in high school students in a hypermedia tutoring environment in an attempt to observe behaviors related to help seeking. The results of this study showed that the types of questions (cognitive vs. contextual) asked by students reflected the conceptual gains reported by students on posttest assessments. Cognitive help seeking questions included clarifying ideas, confirming understanding, and engaging in task-based inquiries, whereas contextual help-seeking questions included requests for assistance in navigating the hypermedia environment. The findings suggest that students who made the most gains in posttest relative to pretest assessments, had asked significantly more cognitive help seeking questions related to the content than to the environment.

Almost all technologies can provide some type of on-demand help or support for learners. On-demand help ranges from context-specific hints (e.g., the green or red underlines that a word processor produces when it thinks you have a spelling or grammatical error) to embedded support such as hyperlinks to background material, online glossaries and tutorials. However, research has revealed that learners often fail to make use of these help features, either by not using them effectively or by totally ignoring them (Aleven et al., 2003). Additionally, not all ways of seeking help are equally conducive to learning, and not all technology help-seeking features are well designed. In fact, different types of technologies or technology features can offer different types of support or help to learners.

For example, research has revealed that ILT content creation and delivery tools and collaborative and communication tools were particularly useful in supporting help seeking. The results of a study conducted by Dabbagh and Kitsantas (2005) revealed that using content creation and delivery tools to post sample projects, examples of assignment solutions, and content-specific resources on the course website enabled students to determine the scope and comprehensiveness of the learning task in order to set appropriate goals and seek help as needed. Additionally, the study revealed that the discussion forum feature of collaborative and communication tools was perceived to be useful primarily in supporting help seeking while students were completing assignments. Specifically, the discussion feature allowed students to seek help in understanding the readings by viewing others' postings. Hence ILT can provide both social and nonsocial help-seeking sources.

Moreover, research has revealed that the pedagogical approach supported by a specific technology system impacts the type of help seeking that the technology provides (Aleven et al., 2003). For example, directive and bounded technology systems, such as CAI (Computer-Assisted Instruction) and ITS (Intelligent Tutoring Systems) are more effective at providing context-sensitive or adaptive help relative to the task at hand. Alternatively, open-ended or collaborative technologies (e.g., social networking tools) are more effective at providing formal and informal social sources of help by supporting a community of practice or a learning community.

In fact, there is a lot of research supporting the idea that online learning communities help students develop a social context of rapport, collegiality, and shared meanings (Dabbagh & Bannan-Ritland, 2005). This sense of community is also promoted through strong interpersonal ties that provide support for learning as well as prevent feelings of isolation in an online environment. Helping students view learning as a collective effort and build a sense of community can greatly promote and support help-seeking practices, especially in students with self-esteem and self-efficacy issues.

For example, Haythornthwaite et al. (2000) investigated students' perceptions of the characteristics of a learning community as well as who and what contributes to a sense of community in a graduate library education program experience. The program consisted of an initial two-week face-to-face experience and thereafter relied primarily on online communication. Overall, the researchers found that students perceived initial community building as a shared experience established with the face-to-face component of the program and maintained throughout by online communication. Specifically, students in the online component of the program provided each other with social and emotional support as well as multiple resources to create a safe, reciprocal and trusting learning environment. However, a few students, who failed to make social or educational community connections, were distressed and found it difficult to overcome a sense of isolation attributable to the lack of face-to-face contact with the instructor and other students. The lack of social cues in the online environment and reduced feedback related to their input created a sense of insecurity for these students as to the appropriateness of their contributions.

Additionally, in the same study, students perceived that maintaining a community through online interaction required more effort than doing so in traditional face-to-face situations. As students engaged with other students and faculty, they moved from isolation to full membership in the community. The students reported that disengaging or "fading back" from online communication was fairly easy to do and that regular synchronous communication (chat whispering, real-time lecturing, whiteboard use) prevented fading back as well as feelings of isolation, and contributed to maintaining community. Haythornthwaite et al.'s (2000) study underscores the importance of providing enhanced social interaction through a range of collaborative and communication tools in order to promote a sense of community and a supportive educational experience for all participants.

Overall, the results of this research suggests that ILT can be effectively used to support and promote help seeking and reduce the perceived threat that inhibits some students from seeking help in face-to-face learning contexts or disengaging in online learning contexts. Dabbagh and Kitsantas (2009) examined how expert instructors used ILT to support and promote help seeking in their courses. The results supported previous research findings (Dabbagh & Kitsantas, 2005) indicating that ILT content creation and delivery tools and collaborative and communication tools were most frequently used by expert instructors to support help seeking. Table 8.2 provides examples of how expert instructors used ILT to support and promote help seeking in online and distributed learning environments.

Training Students to Become Proactive Help Seekers

Instructors can use ILT content creation and delivery tools and collaborative and communication tools to model effective help-seeking behaviors and strategies. For example, Cassandra the instructor in the chapter scenario, could develop a video of herself having difficulty solving a chemistry problem that students will encounter on the test. In this video, she demonstrates what she would do to seek help from both social and nonsocial sources. She also writes down questions for which she would like answers, demonstrating the importance of the question-and-answer format in seeking help. She posts the video on the course website and asks students to view the video and observe the help-seeking process she used to solve the chemistry problem.

In addition, Cassandra uses the discussion forum feature of the LMS and divides the class into groups of five, providing a private discussion forum area for each group. She asks each group to develop a video portraying how the group members would collaborate on solving a chemistry problem. She assigns each group one of four types of problems that are very important in understanding basic chemistry principles, knowing that most

TABLE 8.2   Instructors' Use of ILT to Support Help Seeking

Type of help seeking support	Examples of ILT use to support help seeking
Help students access course material	• "I use the LMS resources tool to post links to web-based or text resources." • "I use the LMS course documents tool to post PPT slides and online lectures." • "I use the LMS links tool to post links to the textbook publisher's website for additional reading material."
Help students locate information about the course requirements	• "I use the LMS syllabus tool to upload the syllabus, which contains all this information." • "I use the LMS assignments tool to post all assignment instructions and rubrics." • "I use the LMS pages organizer tool to structure the course content into a menu that helps students find this information." • "I use the LMS calendar tool to help students easily find assignment due dates and exam dates."
Help students ask the instructor and or classmates a question	• "I use the LMS discussion board to create a question-and-answer area where students can post general questions and receive answers from the instructor or classmates." • "I use e-mail to engage in frequent e-mail exchanges with my students." • "I use the LMS announcements feature to address common questions and the LMS chat feature for specific questions." • "I use the LMS bulletin board tool, which allows students to ask me or fellow-students questions about assignments or concepts." • "I ask students to post questions on their blogs and I also use e-mail and chat to address their questions."
Help students find existing and additional resources on what is being taught in the course	• "I use the LMS resources tool to post links to tutorials and search engines that students can use to find additional information." • "I use the LMS documents feature to post directions for the assignments, which explain how to find related research." • "I use the LMS links tool to create a section that provides suggested reading and/or help for concepts being taught in the course." • "I use the LMS main discussion board to post supplementary articles."

students will not yet know how to solve these problems without seeking appropriate help. She emphasizes that each group should emulate both social and nonsocial help-seeking techniques similar to those she demonstrated in her video. She also creates a class wiki and requires that each group upload their video to the wiki so that all students can view these videos.

Cassandra then picks ten videos and plays them in class, asking students to use Clickers, the wireless response system, to rate the degree to which the group in each video used help-seeking strategies effectively. She then displays the responses on a screen and uses them to provide her own coaching and feedback on help-seeking strategies.

Finally, Cassandra assigns a homework assignment using the LMS assignment tool. The assignment requires that students not only submit the solution to the chemistry problem but to also describe what help-seeking strategies they used to arrive at the solution. This approach will help the instructor guide the students further if needed. Students are then expected to take control of their own help seeking and be able to become adaptive help seekers, in effect knowing how, why, and when to ask for help and what type of help is most useful for the task.

Conclusion

This chapter described how instructors can support and promote effective help seeking in college students. It provided examples of how instructors can use ILT to establish an atmosphere of trust and foster a give-and-take approach to leaning. This approach ensures that students who fear embarrassment, perceived threat, or have low self-esteem and self-efficacy beliefs can seek help when needed and become adaptive help seekers.

References

Aleven, V., McLaren, B., Roll, I., & Koedinger, K. (2004). Towards tutoring help seeking: Applying cognitive modeling top meta-cognitive skills. *Proceedings of the 7th International Conference on Intelligent Tutoring Systems* (ITS-2004).

Aleven, V., Stahl, E., Schworm, S, Fischer, F., & Wallace, R. (2003). Help seeking and help design in interactive learning environments. *Review of Educational Research, 73*(3), 277–320.

Butler, D. L., & Winne, P. H. (1995). Feedback and self-regulated learning: A theoretical synthesis. *Review of Educational Research, 65*(3), 245–281.

Dabbagh, N. (2003). Scaffolding: An important teacher competency in online learning. *TechTrends for Leaders in Education and Training, 47*(2), 39–44.

Dabbagh, N., & Bannan-Ritland, B. (2005). *Online learning: Concepts, strategies, and application.* Upper Saddle River, NJ: Prentice-Hall Pearson Education.

Dabbagh, N., & Kitsantas, A. (2005). Using Web-based pedagogical tools as scaffolds for self-regulated learning. *Instructional Science, 33,* 513–540.

Dabbagh, N., & Kitsantas, A. (2009). *How do experienced online instructors use Integrative Learning Technologies (ILT) to support student self-regulation and learning?* Unpublished manuscript, George Mason University, Fairfax, VA.

Godbole-Chaudhuri, P., Winters, F. I., Azevedo, R., & Hoffman, N. (2006, June). Help-seeking behavior and learning with hypermedia. *Proceedings of the 7th International Conference on Learning Sciences,* International Society of the Learning Sciences.

Haythornthwaite, C., Kazmer, M., Robins, J., & Shoemaker, S. (2000). Community development among distance learners: Temporal and technological dimensions. *Journal of Computer-Mediated Communication, 6*(1). Retrieved September 27, 2008 from: http://jcmc.indiana.edu/vol6/issue1/haythornthwaite.html

Karabenick, S. A. (2001). Seeking help in large college classes: Who, why, and from whom? *New perspectives on help seeking as an adaptive, strategic resource of self-regulated learners.* Symposium conducted at the annual meeting of the American Educational Research Association (AERA), Seattle, WA.

Karabenick, S. A., & Knapp, J. R. (1991). Relationship of academic help seeking to the use of learning strategies and other instrumental achievement behavior in college students. *Journal of Educational Psychology, 83,* 221–230.

Karabenick, S. A., & Knapp, J. R. (1998). *Help seeking in academic settings: Goals, groups, and contexts.* Mahwah, NJ: Lawrence Erlbaum Associates.

Kitsantas, A., & Chow, A. (2007). College students' perceived threat and preference for seeking help in traditional, distributed and distance learning environments. *Computers and Education, 48*(3), 383–395.

Knapp, J. R., & Karabenick, S. A. (1988). Incidence of formal and informal help-seeking in higher education. *Journal of College Student Development, 29,* 233–227.

Newman, R. S. (2008). The motivational role of adaptive help seeking in self-regulated learning. In D. H. Schunk and B. J. Zimmerman (Eds.), *Motivation and self-regulated learning: Theory, research, and applications* (pp. 315–338). New York: Lawrence Erlbaum Associates.

Newman, R. S., & Goldin, L. (1990). Children's reluctance to seek help with schoolwork. *Journal of Educational Psychology, 82,* 92–100.

Perrine, R. M., Lisle, J., & Tucker, D. L. (1995). Effects of a syllabus offer of help, student age, and class size on college students' willingness to seek support from faculty. *Journal of Experimental Education, 64,* 41–52.

Ryan, A. M., & Pintrich, P. R. (1997). Should I ask for help? The role of motivation and attitudes in adolescents' help seeking in math class. *Journal of Educational Psychology, 89,* 329–341.

Ryan, A. M., Pintrich, P. R., & Midgley, C. (2001). Avoiding seeking help in the classroom: Who and why? *Educational Psychology Review, 13*, 93–114.

Smith, P., & Ragan, T. (1999). *Instructional Design.* Upper Saddle River, NJ: Prentice-Hall.

Tardy, C. H. (1992). Assessing the functions of supportive messages: Experimental studies of social support. *Communication research, 19*(2), 175–192.

9

Motivation, Affect, and Learning Communities

Contents

Learning to Learn with Integrative Learning Technologies, pages 143–157
Copyright © 2010 by Information Age Publishing
All rights of reproduction in any form reserved.

Scenario

Those are able who think they are able.

—Virgil

D ante and Zander are both students in a large introductory English writing course. The course involves intensive writing and weekly assignments on various topics designed to improve student writing skills. Although English is particularly challenging both for these students, who are nonnative speakers, Dante seems interested in the course and has expressed a goal to improve his writing. The instructor, Maria had noticed that Dante seems confident that he can do well in the course. Dante has also taken responsibility for correcting mistakes in response to feedback on assignments. Consequently, his writing performance has already shown signs of improvement after only a couple of weeks.

On the other hand, Zander appears to be bored during class and his assignments seem to be hastily completed and are full of errors. When Maria approaches Zander and attempts to provide corrective feedback, he seems to listen; however, his assignments continue to display the same errors. Zander seems to lack the desire to improve his writing, yet as his instructor Maria understands that Zander's academic and professional success depends on strong writing skills. Maria wants to help Zander succeed in the course—but what can she do if he is not willing to try?

Maria decides to apply several strategies from her training in motivation to prompt Zander's and other students' interest. First, she decides to allow students to choose their topic for the next writing assignment. Next, she forms collaborative writing groups among students. She also asks each group to formulate a list of steps required to complete each goal. Maria also facilitates online discussions on the characteristics and potential outcomes of possessing strong writing skills, allowing students to share personal experiences of success in writing. Essentially she creates a learning community to support identity building and foster communication and collaboration.

What Are Motivation, Affect, and Learning Communities?

Academic motivation is a process by which students are able to sustain and instigate goal-directed behavior (Schunk, Pintrich, & Meece, 2008). This concept presumes that the student is an active participant, rather than a passive observer, in the learning experience. On the other hand, affect refers to the student's emotions and feelings, including affective reactions such as likes and dislikes, and emotions such as frustration, happiness, and anger. Learning communities (also referred to as knowledge-building communities or communities of practice) are groups of people who support each other in their learning agendas, working together on projects, learning from one another as well as from their environment, and engaging in a collective sociocultural experience in which participation is transformed into a new experience or new knowledge (Rogoff, 1994; Wilson & Ryder, 1998). As a result, learning communities can act as academic and social support structures that allow students to learn in more authentic, engaging, and challenging ways, thus fostering motivation and positive affect.

Research on Motivation, Affect, and Learning Communities: Implications for Instruction

Motivation

Motivational strategies include the use of strategies and tactics to enhance extrinsic motivation for a task such as engaging in positive self-talk, or creating self-rewards for completing a task (Pintrich, 2004). For example, a student who is studying for an important final exam can regulate his or her test anxiety by telling himself or herself, "Don't worry about how you will do on the test, just study," and regulate motivation by telling himself or herself, "Yes, I know this stuff!" Learners can also increase their motivation to complete boring or distasteful tasks through the use of strategies to make the task more interesting or meaningful. Students have reported using many creative ways to achieve their learning goals, including making the task relevant to their lives in some way or through maintaining a mastery-oriented focus on learning (Pintrich, 2004). Most important, an individuals' motivational state, affect, and subsequent actions are proposed to be a result of his or her beliefs and not based on objective reality (Bandura, 1997). A key construct of motivation and an important determiner of affect is self-efficacy.

Overall, self-efficacy is a powerful motivational belief that influences virtually all aspects of a person's life (Pajares, 2008). More specifically, self-efficacy is defined as the belief one holds regarding his or her capability to organize and implement action to complete a specific task. Self-efficacy beliefs are context and domain-specific and are the main force for action (Bandura, 1997). They influence the effort and persistence an individual will expend on a task and also dictate the level of perseverance in the face of obstacles. It should be noted that an individual's self-efficacy beliefs are malleable and can increase as a result of intervention.

High self-efficacy beliefs have been found to be associated with greater academic success and achievement in numerous studies (Bruinsma, 2004; Chemers, Hu, & Garcia, 2001; Robbins et al., 2004). For example, in a meta-analysis of 109 studies, Robbins et al. (2004) found that among nine psychological constructs (achievement motivation, academic goals, institutional commitment, perceived social support, social involvement, academic self-efficacy, general self-concept, academic-related skills, and contextual influences), academic self-efficacy was the strongest predictor of GPA. Self-efficacy also influences students' use of more-effective strategies and higher intrinsic interest in learning activities (Zimmerman, 2006). Regardless of the current skill level, students with higher self-efficacy have a higher likelihood of successfully achieving a task than students with lower self-efficacy. Specifically, when students think that their effort and action will produce the desired result, they are more likely to adapt more effective strategies and persist to overcome academic difficulties.

Additionally, self-efficacy beliefs as a motivational construct directly influence how students self-regulate their cognitions and behaviors to meet academic goals. Hence motivational and self-regulatory constructs are intimately and cyclically related (Zimmerman, 2006). For example, students with high self-efficacy beliefs will adopt goals that are mastery-oriented and use more effective strategies to excel than will students with low self-efficacy beliefs (Pajares, 2008). Self-efficacy also influences other self-regulatory processes such as self-monitoring and self-evaluation (Zimmerman, 2000). Students with a positive sense of efficacy use high personal standards to monitor and evaluate their own work and choose to adopt more challenging goals (Pajares, 2008).

Another key construct of motivation that is fostered through self-reactive and self-efficacy mechanisms is intrinsic interest (Bandura, 1997). Intrinsic interest has been defined as the enjoyment and satisfaction experienced by an individual during a task or the individual's interest in the content of the subject matter (Schunk et al., 2008). In fact, intrinsic interest is more about the enjoyment of being involved in a task than about the outcome associated with the task. Students who are intrinsically motivated to engage in certain tasks are typically characterized as students who prefer challenging as opposed to simple tasks; work hard for their own personal satisfaction and not for the praise or expectations of others; attempt to work independently and actively with little assistance from the teacher; judge and evaluate their own work rather than relying on feedback they receive from the teacher;

and use more internal, adaptive attributions than external attributions for their successes and failures (Harter & Connell, 1984). As a result, these students are more likely to show high levels of engagement, persistence, and motivation (Wigfield & Eccles, 1992).

Affect

Affect plays an important role in the learning process, along with cognitions, behavior, and the environment (Schutz & Lanehart, 2002; Schunk et al., 2008). For example, it has been suggested that affect and information are linked in an associative network during memory processes such as retrieval and storage (Forgas, 2000). Specifically, researchers have found that students are better able to recall information that was emotionally charged (e.g., talking about the atrocities of World War II or the experience of American slaves during the pre-Civil War era) than information that was nonemotional (Bower & Forgas, 2001).

Furthermore, negative emotions such as fear and anxiety can overload the attentional capacity of a learner to engage cognitively as well as result in decreased interest and motivation; whereas positive emotions related to learner satisfaction and enjoyment can enhance intrinsic interest and motivation (Schunk et al., 2008). Pekrun (1992) proposed a general taxonomy of emotions related to student learning, motivation, and achievement. Within this taxonomy, emotions are categorized according to positive or negative dimensions and whether they represent task-related or social emotions. Task-related emotions are those that are relevant to achievement or learning activities in school or work environments. In contrast, social emotions are posited to be related to interactions between individuals in social settings. Pekrun (1992) further distinguished task-related emotions into prospective, process-related, and retrospective. These three elements attempt to identify the different emotions that students may come across before, during, and after the completion of a task. Specifically, prospective emotions are the different anticipations that the student may have about the outcome of the task, or emotions felt before engaging in the task. Process-related emotions are the student's feelings while engaged in the task. Retrospective emotions are the emotions that the student may experience after the task is completed. Generally, more positive emotions across these three task-related distinctions are related to more adaptive motivational, self-regulatory, and achievement outcomes. An understanding of the taxonomy of emotions that Pekrun (1992) proposed allows instructors to target any one of these factors to help students increase motivation, self-regulation, and achievement.

Affect is also related to motivation through goals and self-efficacy beliefs. If students set appropriate goals to accomplish and have a positive set of competence beliefs, they are more likely to feel cheerful rather than depressed (Bandura, 1997). Additionally, students will react emotionally to their successes and failures. In fact, students will be happier for their successes if they did not expect success and similarly, students will be more ashamed or depressed for their failures if they did not expect to fail. However, these emotions depend on how students analyze and interpret their successes and failures. For example, if students attribute their failures to their own shortcomings (e.g., "I'm just not smart enough to do well"), they may feel depressed or upset. However, if students attribute their failures to the shortcomings of the environment (e.g., "The testing room was so cold and distracting") they may feel angry or frustrated. Overall, positive emotions have been found to be associated with creativity and deep-level processing, while negative emotions promote the use of aversive or avoidance approaches, low-efficacy beliefs, external attributions, and surface level-strategies (Schunk et al., 2008). In summary, motivation and affect are critical elements in student learning and achievement.

Learning Communities

Learning communities can help support and promote motivation and positive affect and in turn foster student self-regulation and achievement. Learning communities transcend classroom boundaries and promote the social construction of knowledge, active learning, and interactions between faculty and students and among students. Learning communities also encourage diverse perspectives and the integration and synthesis of knowledge. Specifically, the purpose of a learning community is to (a) develop members' capabilities and skills, thereby enhancing their self-efficacy beliefs; (b) build and exchange knowledge in a relevant and meaningful context; and (c) create a supportive learning environment that promotes students motivational beliefs and intrinsic interest (Schrum & Berenfeld, 1997; Stefanou & Salisbury-Glennon, 2002).

In academic settings, learning communities represent an intentional restructuring of students' time, credit, and learning experiences around an interdisciplinary theme to foster more explicit intellectual and emotional connections among students, between students and faculty, and across disciplines (MacGregor et al., 1999). Additionally, undergraduate learning communities are proposed to be an effective way to encourage academic and social integration (Shapiro & Levine, 1999; Stefanou & Salisbury-Glennon, 2002). This integration is important since developmental theorists have found that cognitive and affective components of learning are intertwined and cannot be separated. Learning communities are premised on this integration and support learning as a social process that emphasizes meaningful activity through social interaction (Dabbagh & Bannan-Ritland, 2005).

Learning communities are also purported to enhance motivation for deeper-level cognitive processing and to foster greater persistence and effort during learning (Ames, 1992). Given that student cognitive and affective dimensions of learning are intertwined, learning communities should be designed to enhance both of these dimensions. This includes providing students with tasks that are challenging but attainable, and finding a way to intrinsically motivate students, arouse their interest, and create and maintain their curiosity. Stefanou and Salisbury-Glennon (2002) investigated the role of learning communities in student motivation and the use of strategies in first-semester freshmen. The researchers incorporated integrated courses, active and collaborative learning, learning technologies, and library resources, and trained instructors through workshops to develop learning communities. The results showed significant changes in motivation and strategy use in posttest assessments. For example, students reported significant increases in intrinsic and extrinsic motivation, greater internal control over their learning, higher self-efficacy, and significantly lower levels of test-related anxiety. In terms of strategy use, significant increases were reported for rehearsal strategies, organization strategies, critical thinking, time management, help seeking, and collaborative learning. The question then is, How can instructors design learning communities that motivate students to engage in learning as productive, open-minded, and supportive members?

Researchers have suggested several guidelines to developing effective and engaging learning communities. For example, Shapiro and Levine (1999) proposed that when designing learning communities for first-year college students, faculty should organize students into small groups, help students create academic and social support networks, help students focus on learning outcomes, and provide a setting for community-based delivery of academic support programs. Additionally, Dabbagh and Bannan-Ritland (2005) suggested that instructors should ensure that the following pedagogical characteristics are incorporated in the design of a learning community (p. 176):

- control of learning is distributed among the participants in the community and is not in the hands of a single instructor or expert;
- participants are committed to the generation and sharing of new knowledge;
- learning activities are flexible and negotiated;

- participants exhibit high levels of dialogue, interaction, collaboration, and social negotiation;
- a shared goal, problem, or project binds the participants and provides a common focus and an incentive to work together as a community;
- an appreciation of diversity, multiple perspectives and epistemic issues;
- traditional disciplinary and conceptual boundaries are crossed; and
- innovation and creativity are encouraged and supported.

Furthermore, researchers (Dabbagh & Bannan-Ritland, 2005; Dennen, 2000; Koschmann, 1996; Rennie & Mason, 2004; Winn & Bricken, 1992) have argued that technology can be used effectively to create engaging learning communities. For example, Carswell et al. (2000) found that students perceived the use of the Internet to be a convenient learning delivery mechanism that (a) increased interaction with other students and the instructor; (b) enabled more timely feedback on assignments; and (c) provided learning opportunities beyond the course, such as the ability to share issues with other students and expand Internet skills. This study provided evidence that the use of technology can motivate students to learn and collaborate, which are essential elements of an effective learning community. Given these research findings, how can instructors use Integrative Learning Technologies (ILT) to design learning communities that promote motivation and positive affect?

Supporting and Promoting Motivation and Affect in Learning Communities Using ILT

Overall, social media and social networking tools (e.g., weblogs, wikis, Facebook, LinkedIn), which constitute a subset of ILT, are ideal technologies for creating effective and engaging learning communities. Additionally, other ILT categories (e.g., collaborative and communication tools, content creation and delivery tools, and learning tools) can be used to design learning tasks that support and promote motivation and affect in learning communities. Examples of such learning tasks include exploratory, dialogic, and supportive. More specifically, exploratory learning tasks (also called experiential learning tasks) engage students in problem-solving activities that require the exploration of a variety of resources to gather relevant information pertaining to the problem at hand (Dabbagh & Bannan-Ritland,

2005). Through exploration, students learn how to set achievable learning goals and manage the pursuit of those goals (Collins, 1991).

Dialogic learning tasks, on the other hand, emphasize social interaction through dialogue and conversation. The idea is to assist learners in constructing new knowledge primarily through dialogue as a form of interaction. Examples of dialogic learning tasks include articulation, reflection, promoting multiple perspectives, collaboration, and social negotiation. Supportive learning tasks are typically initiated by the expert, coach, mentor, or instructor, with the goal of modeling the desired performance, skill, or process, and observing and supporting learners during their execution of a learning task. Overall, exploratory, dialogic, and supportive learning tasks can be very effective in promoting and supporting motivation and positive affect in learning communities because they situate learning in realistic and relevant contexts and engage students in social interaction. Moreover, they encourage ownership of learning and nurture self-awareness of the knowledge construction process (Driscoll, 2000). Table 9.1 provides examples of how ILT categories and features can be used to develop exploratory, dialogical, and supportive learning tasks.

TABLE 9.1 Promoting Exploratory, Dialogical, and Supportive Learning Tasks Using ILT

Type of learning task	Example of learning task	ILT category or tool
Exploratory	• Develop an authentic case, scenario, or problem	• ILT content creation and delivery tools (e.g., web publishing or resource sharing tools) or social media (e.g., podcast, vodcast)
	• Create discipline specific simulations, microworlds, and webquests to engage students in hypothesis generation	• ILT content creation and delivery tools (specifically, instructional design tools embedded in LMS)
	• Provide search tools, note-taking tools, resource tools, and help tools to support student exploration of relevant information and resources required to solve a problem	• ILT learning tools
Dialogical	• Require students to reflect on their understanding of content or topics of interest and/or to analyze their performance against a rubric by journaling	• ILT collaborative and communication tools or social media (e.g., weblogs, discussion forum)

(continued)

TABLE 9.1   Promoting Exploratory, Dialogical, and Supportive Learning Tasks Using ILT (continued)

Type of learning task	Example of learning task	ILT category or tool
	• Create a structured discussion requiring students to debate an issue as a group or class to promote articulation	• ILT collaborative and communication tools (e.g., discussion forum)
	• Set up a class wiki to enable collaborative group work promoting collaboration and social negotiation	• ILT collaborative and communication tools or social media (e.g., wiki)
Supportive	• Use virtual sessions to model thinking processes aloud while students are observing	• ILT collaborative and communication tools (e.g., Adobe Connect)
	• Videotape a demonstration of how an expert solves a problem or makes critical decisions in a real-world situation	• ILT content creation and delivery tools or social media (e.g., YouTube)
	• Provide one-on-one coaching while students are working on an assignment	• ILT collaborative and communication tools (e.g., chat tools)
	• Provide sequenced and modular instruction to scaffold students who need a structured learning environment	• ILT content creation and delivery tools (e.g., LMS-embedded design tools)

Training Students to Become Motivated Learners Through Learning Communities

In the last section of this chapter we demonstrate how the English instructor, Maria, in the chapter scenario can design a learning community using ILT to help students like Zander regulate their motivation and affect. First, Maria finds a few documentaries on YouTube about the lives of renowned and successful writers (e.g., J. K. Rowling) to gain students' interest and attention and stimulate their curiosity in the topic. Maria selects writers whose work aligns with her freshmen's culture to ensure that students will be able to relate to these writers. She posts the links to these documentaries to the course wiki.

Next, Maria provides a variety of topics that students can choose from. She organizes these topics and related online resources using the social bookmarking tool Delicious. Additionally, Maria informs her students that they can choose their own paper topic if they do not like the choices provided. She provides links to several websites that allow students to search for writing topics using relevant keywords. This helps a student like Zander select a topic that he is familiar with. In essence, Maria has designed exploratory learning tasks using ILT content creation and delivery tools and social media to help students, particularly those who are less motivated or interested, take ownership of the learning process—a key principle of a learning community.

Furthermore, in order to help students build self-efficacy so that they feel capable of engaging in the writing process, Maria breaks down the writing assignment into small, proximal, and attainable goals (first submit a topic of interest, next submit an outline, then submit a draft, and so on). Additionally, as Maria monitors each student's progress toward achieving these goals, she provides words of encouragement through e-mail as well as in person. Essentially, Maria has engaged in a supportive learning task by scaffolding students to successfully complete the writing assignment.

Next, using wiki software (e.g., pbwiki.com), Maria creates virtual student groups based on their writing topics and asks each group to (a) select a name that best reflects their writing genre (e.g., fiction, nonfiction, documentary, autobiography, romance, fables), (b) post a group picture to the wiki, and (c) assemble 20 resources related to their writing genre using Delicious. Then she posts an online article about a controversial topic and asks each group to develop a position statement. These collaborative activities are examples of dialogic learning tasks that support interaction and social negotiation, another key principle of a learning community. Maria provides feedback (a supportive learning task) on the viability of each group's position statement and the credibility of the resources the group has assembled about their writing genre.

Furthermore, Maria posts a writing rubric and template to the class wiki. The rubric and template are very clear in depicting exactly how the individual writing assignment will be graded and what is expected with respect to length, formatting, peer feedback, and other collaborative activities. She then asks each student to begin the writing assignment on his or her own, based on the approved topic of choice. She also uploads exemplary papers from past courses using ILT content creation and delivery tools and provides a timeline for submitting writing drafts. Maria models for students how to provide peer feedback by offering her own feedback on first drafts using the comments and review features in Word. Maria is careful to praise students when they have demonstrated good writing skills and offers concrete suggestions for improvement. Maria also informs the class that each group has the option of posting their papers to a website that promotes student writers in order to have their papers evaluated by a well-known writer. By doing this, she is providing incentives to generate intrinsic motivation in the topic.

In this example, Maria has successfully created a virtual learning community by designing exploratory, dialogic, and supportive learning tasks around the course objectives and assignments. She primarily used social networking tools and ILT content creation and delivery tools to design this learning community. In addition to integrating key principles of learning communities, Maria was able to motivate her students. Table 9.2 provides additional examples of how instructors can use ILT to assist students in regulating motivation and affect in learning communities.

TABLE 9.2 Regulating Motivation and Affect Using ILT

Motivation and affect constructs	Use of ILT to regulate motivation	ILT category or tool
Self-efficacy	Provide students with a scale that assesses self-efficacy beliefs for writing (or any other skill) and instruct students to use the scale to examine how their self-efficacy beliefs change as they apply assigned strategies	Assessment tools (e.g., an online survey tool such as SurveyMonkey)
Extrinsic/ intrinsic motivation	Create tasks that are challenging yet feasible and achievable, and provide students with incentives to present their work and to have their work evaluated by experts	Content creation and delivery tools (e.g., audio and video sharing tools)
Task-related emotions	Provide students with the opportunity to submit multiple writing drafts and give timely and supportive feedback to encourage students to reflect upon and improve performance	Content creation and delivery tools (e.g., weblogs and wikis)
Social emotions	Provide students with collaborative learning opportunities and peer-to-peer interaction to minimize negative social emotions such as jealousy, envy, and antipathy, and maximize empathy and gratitude	Collaborative and communication tools (e.g., discussion forums and online group work areas)

Conclusion

This chapter described the role of motivation and affect in student learning. It also addressed how learning communities can be designed to cultivate positive affect and motivational beliefs in students. In particular, the chapter described how instructors can use ILT to develop different types of learning tasks that can enhance these processes in a learning community. Examples of these learning tasks included exploratory, dialogical, and supportive.

References

Ames, C. (1992). Classrooms: Goals, structures, and student motivation. *Journal of Educational Psychology, 84*, 261–271.

Bandura, A. (1997). *Self-efficacy: The exercise of control.* New York: Freeman & Company.

Bower, G. H., & Forgas. J. P. (2001). Mood and social memory. In J. P. Forgas (Ed), *Handbook of affect and social cognition* (pp. 95–120). Mahwah, NJ: Erlbaum.

Bruinsma, M. (2004). Motivation, cognitive processing and achievement in higher education. *Learning and Instruction, 11*(6), 549–568.

Carswell, L., Thomas, P., Petre, M., Price, B., & Richards, M. (2000). Distance education via the Internet: The student experience. *British Journal of Educational Technology, 31*(1), 29–46.

Chemers, M., Hu, L., & Garcia, B. F. (2001). Academic self-efficacy and first-year college student performance adjustment. *Journal of Educational Psychology, 93*(1), 55–64.

Collins, A. (1991). Cognitive apprenticeship and instructional technology. In L. Idol & B. F. Jones (Eds.), *Educational values and cognitive instruction: Implications for reform* (pp. 121–131). Hillsdale, NJ: Erlbaum.

Dabbagh, N., & Bannan-Ritland, B. (2005). *Online learning: Concepts, strategies, and application.* Upper Saddle River, NJ: Prentice-Hall.

Dennen, V. P. (2000). Task structuring for on-line problem based learning: A case study. *Educational Technology & Society 3*(3). Retrieved July 14, 2007 from: http://www.ifets.info/journals/3_3/d08.html

Driscoll, M. P. (2000). *Psychology of learning for instruction* (2nd ed.). Needham Heights, MA: Allyn & Bacon.

Forgas, J. (2000). The role of affect in social cognition. In J. Forgas (Ed.), *Feeling and thinking: The role of affect in social cognition* (pp. 1–28). New York: Cambridge University Press.

Harter, S., & Connell, J. P. (1984). A comparison of children's achievement and related self-perceptions of competence, control, and motivational orientation. In J. G. Nicholls (Ed.), *Advances in motivation and achievement: The development of achievement motivation* (Vol. 3, pp. 219–250). Greenwich, CT: JAI Press.

Koschmann, T. (1996). Paradigm shifts and instructional technology: An introduction. In T. Koschmann (Ed.), *CSCL: Theory and practice of an emerging paradigm* (pp. 1–23). Mahwah, NJ: Erlbaum.

MacGregor, J., Smith, B. L., Tinto, V., & Levine, J. H. (1999, April 19). *Learning about learning communities: Taking student learning seriously.* Materials prepared for the National Resource Center for the First-Year Experience and Students in Transition Teleconference, Columbia, SC.

Pajares, F. (2008). Motivational role of self-efficacy beliefs in self-regulated learning. In. D. H. Schunk, & B. J. Zimmerman, (Eds.), *Motivation and self-regulated learning* (pp. 111–139). New York: Taylor & Francis Group.

Pekrun, R. (1992). The impact of emotions on learning and achievement: Towards a theory of cognitive and motivational mediators. *Applied Psychology: An International Review, 41,* 359–376.

Pintrich, P. R. (2004). A conceptual framework for assessing motivation and self-regulated learning in college students. *Educational Psychology Review, 16,* 385–407.

Rennie, F., & Mason, R. (2004). *The connecticon: Learning for the connected generation.* Greenwich, CT: Information Age Publishing.

Robbins, S. B., Lauver, K., Le, H., Davis, D., Langley, R., & Carlstrom, A. (2004). Do psychosocial and study skill factors predict college outcomes? A meta-analysis. *Psychological Bulletin, 130*(2), 261–288.

Rogoff, B. (1994). Developing understanding of the idea of communities of learners. *Mind, Culture, and Activity, 4,* 209–229.

Schrum, L., & Berenfeld, B. (1997). *Teaching and learning in the information age.* Boston, MA: Allyn & Bacon.

Schunk, D. H., Pintrich, P. R., Meece, J. L. (2008). *Motivation in education: Theory, research, and applications.* Upper Saddle River, NJ: Pearson-Merrill Prentice-Hall.

Schutz, P. A., & Lanehart, S. L. (2002). Emotions in education: Guest editors' introduction. *Educational Psychologist, 37,* 67–68.

Shapiro, N. S., & Levine, J. (1999). *Creating learning communities: A practical guide to winning support, organizing for change, and implementing programs.* San Francisco: Jossey-Bass.

Stefanou, C. R., & Salisbury-Glennon, J. D. (2002). Developing motivation and cognitive learning strategies through an undergraduate learning community. *Learning Environments Research, 5,* 77–97.

Wigfield, A., & Eccles, J. S. (1992). The development of achievement task values: A theoretical analysis. *Developmental Review, 12,* 265–310.

Wilson, B., & Ryder, M. (1998). Distributed learning communities: An alternative to designed instructional systems. Retrieved July 14, 2007 from: http://carbon.cudenver.edu/~bwilson/dlc.html

Winn, W., & Bricken, W. (1992). Designing virtual worlds for use in mathematics education: The example of experimental algebra. *Educational Technology 32*(12), 12–19.

Zimmerman, B. J. (2000). Attainment of self-regulation: A social cognitive perspective. In M. Boekaerts, P. Pintrich, & M. Zeidner (Eds.), *Self-regulation: Theory, research, and applications* (pp.13–39). Orlando, FL: Academic Press.

Zimmerman, B. J. (2006). Enhancing students' academic responsibility and achievement: A social-cognitive self-regulatory account. In R. J. Sternberg, & R. Subotnik (Eds.), *Optimizing student success in school with the other three Rs: Reasoning, resilience, and responsibility* (pp. 179–197). Greenwich, CT: Information Age.

10

New Approaches to Integrative Learning Technologies

Contents

Learning to Learn with Integrative Learning Technologies, pages 159–178

Copyright © 2010 by Information Age Publishing

159

Scenario

The Net Generation has arrived! Boomers stand back. Already these kids are learning, playing, communicating, working and creating communities very differently than their parents. They are a force for social transformation.

—Don Tapscott (1988)

Steve is a professor in the Instructional Technology program of a large university. When you visit Steve's Web page, you can immediately experience the latest Web 2.0 technologies and how Steve employs these technologies for teaching, learning, and social networking. For starters, his phone number is active, meaning you can dial it instantaneously if you have VoIP (Voice over Internet Protocol) software such as Skype. His e-mail and chat (IM) addresses are also clickable and ready for messaging. More important, there are about 10 icons next to his photograph that represent links to Web 2.0 tools and applications such as a blog, Twitter, Facebook, Friendfeed, Flickr, and Delicious, to name a few. When you click these icons, you can learn about Steve's whereabouts, views and opinions, latest readings and writings, conferences he will be attending, professional and personal groups he has joined, new professional initiatives he is undertaking, causes he is supporting, and a variety of educational resources that he has tagged to create folksonomies of digital resources.

Steve's students consider him a role model when it comes to using Web 2.0 technologies and social software. Steve has a real social presence online and knows how to leverage this presence to support and promote his personal and professional goals. For example, he uses multiple Web 2.0 technologies to promote open education and social learning. So what is it about Web 2.0 technologies that enable such a powerful social and academic presence for a professor? What about Steve's students? Are they also experiencing the social networking power of Web 2.0 technologies? Are they using these technologies to support their own learning? And what is the impact of Web 2.0 technologies on student self-regulation and motivation? Can institutions leverage Web 2.0 tools to create and sustain learning communities that motivate students to learn and succeed academically? Finally, what are some of the challenges of implementing Web 2.0 platforms and applications in higher-education contexts?

What Are Web 2.0 and Social Software?

Integrative Learning Technologies (ILT) are defined in Chapter 2 as a dynamic collection or aggregation of Web tools, software applications, and mobile technologies that integrate technological and pedagogical features and affordances of the Internet and the World Wide Web to facilitate the design, development, delivery, and management of online and distributed learning. This definition is broad enough to encompass current and emerging technologies such as Web 2.0 tools and social software as well as more traditional or older Internet and web-based technologies such as Learning Management Systems (LMS). In this final chapter, the focus is exclusively on the learning affordances of Web 2.0 technologies and social software and their role in providing new approaches to using ILT in higher education.

At the time this chapter introduction was written (July 2008), a search on Google for "Web 2.0" returned 95.2 million results. Hence, it should be no surprise that defining Web 2.0 is a difficult task. There is even a Web 2.0 Summit (formerly known as Web 2.0 Conference) that has been convening annually since 2004 in order to stimulate discussion around this rather ambiguous construct. Despite these initiatives, defining just what Web 2.0 means still engenders much disagreement. However there are a few definitions and guiding principles that can be gleaned from the emerging literature and the cyberspace discussions surrounding this relatively new term or construct.

We begin with Tim O'Reilly's definition of Web 2.0 because it was the Vice President of O'Reilly Media Inc., Dale Dougherty, who first coined the term Web 2.0 in 2004 at a conference brainstorming session. In 2005 several related discussions and blogposts took place leading O'Reilly (2006) to finally publish the following "compact" definition:

> Web 2.0 is the business revolution in the computer industry caused by the move to the Internet as platform, and an attempt to understand the rules for success on that new platform. Chief among those rules is this: Build applications that harness network effects to get better the more people use them. This is what I've elsewhere called harnessing collective intelligence.

Another formal attempt at defining Web 2.0 came from the Burton Group report (April 2007) which posited that Web 2.0 is "an ambiguous concept—a conglomeration of folksonomies and syndication, wikis and mash-ups, social networks and reputation, ubiquitous content, and perhaps even kitchen sinks" and that "the value of Web 2.0 can be summarized in two words—participative and collaborative—served with a supersized helping of ubiquitous content" (Lindstrom, 2007, p. 6). Additionally, Davis (2008) characterized Web 2.0 as the "The Social Web" and described it as the second stage of Internet growth that is all about "connecting people" in contrast to "connecting information" (p. 3). Furthermore, Anderson (2007) suggested that delineating between Web 1.0 (i.e., the Web) and Web 2.0 will help us understand the strategic implications of Web 2.0 technologies for higher education. Anderson also stated that Web 2.0 is "more than a set of 'cool' and new technologies and services" and that the so called "network effect" that a billion Internet users are producing is changing the way people interact, do business, and learn (p. 2).

Jones (2008) interviewed 20 Web 2.0 pioneers and influencers, querying them about how they would define Web 2.0. As expected, different perspectives of the term or construct were revealed. However, what stood out were overarching or umbrella themes such as openness, personal experience, software as a service, user-generated content, the people's Web, social networking, social media, grassroots movement, read/write Web, a marketing term that describes the era of the Web we are in right now, wisdom of the crowds, and others.

It is clear from this brief overview that Web 2.0 is a multifaceted and principled construct that it is primarily premised on three perspectives: a business or commercial perspective, a technical or information technology perspective, and a social or people (user) perspective. Our focus in this chapter is on the social or user perspective of Web 2.0 and related technologies and on how higher education faculty can harness Web 2.0 technologies to promote learning how to learn (i.e., self-regulated learning).

The social side of Web 2.0 was emphasized by EDUCAUSE (http://www.educause.edu/) (a nonprofit association whose mission is to advance higher education by promoting the intelligent use of information technology). Specifically, in the 2007 Horizon report (The New Media Consortium & EDUCAUSE Learning Initiative, 2007), the concepts of user-created content and social networking were highlighted as new trends that will have a significant impact on college and university campus learning environments. Due in part to this emphasis, the term *social software* (or *social media*) has become more commonplace in higher education than the term Web 2.0. Additionally, educational researchers and practitioners have further delineated some of the social affordances or attributes of Web 2.0 technologies as (a) establishing group identity and personal reputations, (b) building social contexts of knowledge, (c) enabling personalization, and (d) erecting recommendation and folk knowledge systems (also called folksonomies) (Butterfield, 2003; Sessum, 2006). For example, social networking utilities such as Facebook and LinkedIn enable members to post personal and professional information (e.g., a résumé or CV) and to connect to other professionals and friends with similar interests and skills, forming a personalized network. Members can also ask for endorsements or recommendations from others within their personalized network to establish personal reputation systems. Moreover, employers who become part of the network as individuals can look for specialized talent within this "folk" knowledge system that is entirely built and driven by its members (hence the word *folksonomy*).

However, the degree of qualitative newness of social software and its use in teaching and learning is less than some proclaim. Madden and Fox (2006) concluded in their Pew Internet report that the heart of the Internet has always been its facility for social connectivity and that the actions or affordances that [Web 2.0] technologies enable are "nothing new" when compared to the social sites of the 1990s (p. 5). Additionally, a recent overview of the history of social software (Dabbagh & Reo, 2010) reveals that technologies for networked social interaction have been developmental in nature such that the new Web 2.0-enabled social media are premised on the continuation of older computer-mediated communication (CMC) tools, rather than on a radical transformation of social interaction capabilities as some are proclaiming. From this perspective, Web 2.0 should be seen as a consequence of a more fully implemented Web (Anderson, 2007), or, as "the public acceptance of the fact that the Web is a highly social utility" (Stone, 2008, p. 149). Stone also adds that "for most people there is no Web 2.0, there is just the Web." Despite this evolutionary or developmental perspective, Web 2.0 technologies and in particular social media have changed the nature of social interaction, resulting in a new pedagogical ecology that has implications for higher education and for the use of ILT in supporting and promoting self-regulated learning. We discuss these implications next.

Examples of Social Software: Implications for Instruction

In order to provide specific examples of how social software has impacted teaching and learning in higher education and how professors such as Steve (depicted in the scenario at the beginning of this chapter) are modeling the effective use of social software, we begin by classifying social software into the following six categories:

1. communication tools (e.g., Web 2.0–enabled e-mail applications such as Hotmail, Gmail, and Google Wave; Web conferencing tools such as Adobe Connect; IM tools such as Meebo; and VoIP applications such as Skype)

2. experience- and resource-sharing tools (e.g., blogs, microblogs, & wikis such as WordPress, Twitter, and PBwiki; media sharing tools such as Flickr and YouTube; and social bookmarking tools such as Delicious and Zotero)
3. social networking tools (e.g., LinkedIn, MySpace, Facebook, Plaxo, Ning)
4. immersive virtual worlds (e.g., Second Life, Croquet, and Massive Multiplayer Online Role-Playing Games or MMORPG)
5. Web or online office tools (e.g., Google Apps, Microsoft Office Live, Zoho)
6. mobile technologies (e.g., GPS; digital audio players such as iPod and iTouch; and smart phones such as iPhone and Blackberry)

Figure 10.1 illustrates how these six categories integrate with ILT. Specifically, the inner dashed-dotted circle retains the initial five categories of ILT that were largely premised on Learning Management Systems (LMS) and the outer dashed-dotted circle depicts the new social software categories as an extension of the older ILT categories, emphasizing the developmental or evolutionary perspective of social software.

Individual tools found in these social software categories include a growing number of mostly free digital technologies and social utilities accessible for everyday users on the Web or desktop in a variety of modalities. More specifically, each of the tools or technologies in these two social software categories has features that enable social interaction through various strategies and tactics such as expressing individual identity, gaining awareness of the presence of others, engaging in conversations, establishing relationships, forming groups and reputations, and sharing experiences and resources publicly (Butterfield, 2003; Sessum, 2006). These types of social interactions have affordances for sustaining informal learning communities and enabling the creation of personal and social learning environments or experiences (PLE/SLE). In previous chapters, we provided several examples of how these tools (e.g., blogs, wikis, podcasts) can be used to support and promote specific processes of self-regulated learning such as goal setting, self-monitoring, and help seeking. In this chapter, we provide more comprehensive definitions of selected examples of social software tools and discuss their instructional implications in higher education contexts.

Skype

Skype is considered a Web 2.0 technology and company (Jones, 2008). Listed in the first category of social software tools, Skype is defined as "an

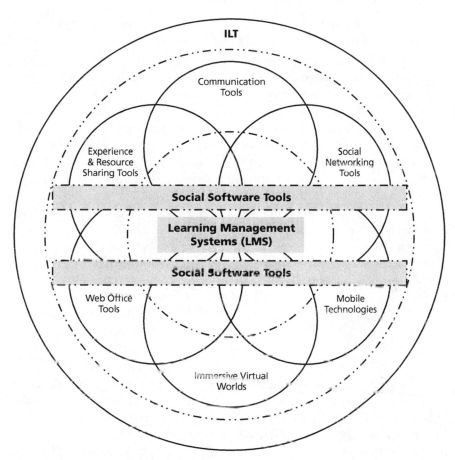

Figure 10.1 ILT and social software tools.

application that turns a personal computer into a telephone" (ELI, 2007). Users are required to download a program to their desktop and create a user account. They can then use the program to talk to any other Skype account holder for free or dial a conventional phone number, including a cell phone, anywhere in the world for a small fee. Skype also allows chatting and video-calling. Skype uses VoIP technology to "convert voice signals into data streams that are sent over the Internet and converted back to audio by the recipient's computer" (ELI, 2007). The technology allows users to make digital recordings of phone conversations which can be very powerful for teaching and learning purposes. Although there are many other similar VoIP applications, Skype's decentralized model (i.e., it does not depend on a central server) allows it to function as a distributed network of computers, giving control of communication to the users and pulling the power of the Internet into their hands.

In terms of uses in higher-education contexts, faculty at some institutions have encouraged students to use Skype to conduct interviews with content experts such as textbook authors, and to collect research data for class projects by conducting and recording interviews with subjects for later analysis. Skype can also be used as a Web conferencing tool, similar to applications that support virtual sessions described in Chapter 2 and other chapters. Audio can be broadcast on speakers, enabling all students in a large class to listen in on an interview, take notes, and ask questions. Skype provides an easy and inexpensive way to deepen student engagement with the content by connecting them with people from all around the world, effectively expanding the walls of the classroom (see ELI, 2007 "7 things you should know about" for more information about Skype and its educational uses). There are also some downsides of using Skype, particularly in academic institutions. Computers that run Skype applications could become relay stations for user calls that consume large bandwidth. Skype also requires access to university networks. This broad access could compromise sensitive information, since such networks are often targets of hackers.

Weblogs

In Chapter 2, we defined a weblog (or blog) as a structured web-based medium for creative expression and journaling. ELI (2007) defines a blog as "an online chronological collection of personal commentary and links." Blogging has become a well-established publishing vehicle, not only for personal diaries and journaling but also for media publications such as editorials on specific topics and political views (ELI, 2007). There are several web-based technologies that support blogging (e.g., WordPress, Blogger). These Web 2.0 technologies also allow bloggers to solicit feedback on their blogposts by embedding a comment feature that enables two-way communication between readers and authors.

Blogging technologies also allow bloggers to post comments to other blogposts on their own blogs and link back to the original blogpost, creating what is called a trackback. "Trackback notifies bloggers when one of their posts is referenced by another blog, making it possible to determine the popularity of a post based on the number and diversity of incoming links to a post" (ELI, 2007). This is one of many technological processes or algorithms used to generate reputation systems. Repeated linking to a blog creates a network or multiplier effect that enhances the reputation and credibility of the blogger. In fact, there is a Web 2.0 site known as Technorati that is dedicated to tracking what is happening in the blogosphere and filtering the good and credible blogposts from the bad blogposts, using reputation and ranking systems. At the time this chapter was written (July 2008), Technorati estimated that 175,000 new blogs were generated every day (Carroll, 2008).

In higher-education contexts, blogs have become an increasingly accepted instructional technology. As described in Chapter 2 and other chapters in this book, blogs can be used to enhance student understanding of content by capturing their chronological reflections (journals) on readings and course topics, enabling self-monitoring and self-evaluation. Additionally, using the trackback feature, students can reference individual blogposts, as they would if they were inserting in-text citations in a paper. Trackback allows students to form rich connections with classmates, content, and experts and peers outside their immediate classroom to create a true learning community.

Overall, blogs can be used as an instructional tool for communication, articulation, reflection, evaluation, and analysis (Dabbagh, 2004). Oravec (2002) posits that blogging encourages students to become more critically analytical in their thinking because others can critique a blog (if it is public) and therefore a student has to stand by his or her opinions. However, blogs also have downsides when viewed in the context of use in higher education (ELI, 2007). Blogs are subjective and unmoderated; hence, the information in a blog cannot be viewed as authoritative. Also, institutions that host blogs may be liable for copyright infringement if the content is not properly attributed. Finally, blogs are transient; institutions may at any time decide to stop hosting them, which could pose problems for those who have linked to those blogs.

Wikis

Wikis are an extremely flexible type of blog that supports collaborative editing on the Web by anyone, at any time, from anywhere (open editing) (Dabbagh, 2004). According to Wikipedia.org, a collaborative encyclopedia and one of the best-known wikis, "a wiki is a collection of Web pages designed to enable anyone who accesses it to contribute or modify content, using a simplified markup language." The key words here are "anyone who accesses it," meaning that wikis allow authors to set access privileges to prevent "anyone" from editing the content. Technically, a wiki is a piece of server software that allows users to create a Web page on the fly using any Web browser for collaborative editing (ELI, 2007). Wikis also have a versioning capability that allows wiki authors to retrieve older versions of the content. Like blogs, wikis allow the integration of multiple media (e.g., graphics, audio, and video), and their significance is that they grow and evolve as a direct result of people's adding to or editing material on the site

(ELI, 2007). However, their most important technological and pedagogical feature is collaborative and open editing across the Internet.

In higher-education contexts, wikis like blogs (but perhaps to a lesser extent) have become an increasingly accepted instructional technology. In Chapter 2 we suggested that faculty use wikis to engage students in collaborative projects that support the creation, editing, and management of content and enable peer and expert feedback. Wikis can also be used as a vehicle for integrating class notes in a course. For example, a college professor used a wiki in her English writing course as a way for students to earn extra credit by posting their notes on related readings (see http://www.oid. ucla.edu/edtech/interviews/lopez/index.html). The task for the students was to use this Web 2.0 technology to create actual Wikipedia pages for the authors they are reading about in order to empower students as authors in their own right.

Overall, wikis are an ideal free and flexible platform for collaborative work. Their multi-user capability, versioning feature, access control, and immediate and simple creation, make them truly conducive to developing PLEs and SLEs. These attributes can also present problems in higher-education contexts. For example, since multiple users can edit the content of a wiki, faculty should monitor the class wiki to ensure the appropriateness of its content. This can be time consuming. Also setting up the initial wiki (navigation, access permission, initial content, purpose, protocols, and so on) can be time consuming. Another factor is that since a wiki is created by a group of users and represents the collective perspective of that group, it has collaborative bias similar to how a blog has individual bias (ELI, 2007). However, this is not necessarily a negative attribute; rather, it often brings out the collective intelligence and identity of a group.

Delicious

Putting it simply, Delicious is a Web 2.0 tool that allows users to store their favorites or bookmarks on the Web rather than on the desktop browser. This is known as social bookmarking and is an important breakthrough for a few reasons. Most significantly, users can access their bookmarks anywhere, anytime, provided there is an Internet connection. Additionally, users can organize, categorize, and classify information in new ways using tags (keywords or descriptors). Joshua Schachter, the founder and creator of Delicious, describes it as a social bookmarking tool because, in addition to storing and tagging your favorite links, using Delicious also allows you to share your bookmarks and to search other people's bookmarks using tags (Schachter, 2008). This functionality could eventually result in a unique keyword structure by a community of users creating a folksonomy (ELI, 2007).

Social bookmarking has multiple educational uses and learning affordances. For example, faculty facilitating collaborative class projects that are research-based can ask student teams to bookmark their resources on the Web using a social bookmarking tool like Delicious, and to organize these resources using keywords that they perceive as meaningful to the topic at hand. If there are five teams in a class and each team has created its own social bookmarking site, a unique folksonomy will emerge about this research topic, creating a rich knowledge base. Additionally, depending on the number and type of keywords these teams use to tag their resources, new relationships among these resources will be formed evolving the knowledge base. New teams can continuously update these folksonomies in future classes by ranking the tags based on their usage frequency and filtering out with the help of the instructor less popular or credible associations in a process similar to that of the trackback feature used in blogs.

An example of a particular folksonomy generated as a result of social bookmarking is Zotero (www.zotero.org). Zotero is a free, open-source research tool that enables scholars to gather, annotate, organize, and share references by means of a Web browser. It was developed by the Center for History and New Media at George Mason University (The New Media Consortium & EDUCAUSE Learning Initiative, 2007). Similar to other social software tools, social bookmarking is a user-generated classification and organization of Web resources. Faculty must continually monitor the content of course-related social bookmarks to ensure that it is credible (ELI, 2007). This is a time-consuming task, not to mention that social bookmarking adds another data location that users have to maintain and update (ELI, 2007).

Facebook

Facebook is a social networking tool or utility that supports social interaction through a dynamic set of networks (ELI, 2007). As described in Chapter 2, social networking tools are also known as community networking tools or group tools and do much more than help build a network of friends. They enable users to find "like-minded folks, establish personal reputations, exchange resources and collaborate" (Alexander, 2006), which is a key principle of social software. Additionally, they enable a connection between knowledge, community, and learning (Shirky, 2003).

In terms of teaching and learning, faculty can guide students to create informal networks that are tailored to their interests and learning needs using social networking tools. These networks eventually become informal learning environments and support systems for building resources and collaboration. Additionally, students can join several existing groups on Facebook and other social networking sites that are specifically geared to their course topics, majors, or professions. For example, if students are studying about e-Learning design, they can find and join several groups or networks on Facebook that center on this topic. Faculty can encourage students to become members of such groups to expand their knowledge of the field, interact with peers and experts, and become members of a community of practice that has lifelong learning implications. Finally, faculty or students can create their own social network using a platform called Ning (Bianchini, 2008). This allows maximum control over design features, type of membership, and educational purpose or goals.

Social networking tools are probably most dangerous in the arena of unintentionally making private information public. Since the number of connections or friends a user has is perceived as a measure of popularity, members often spend a great deal of time online (which in itself can become a problem) to see what their friends are posting on their profiles, what groups their friends are joining, and who their friends are connecting to. This can be extremely distracting and poses the risk of "never-ending wandering with no goal in mind" (ELI, 2007). In addition, if members do not use discretion, they could represent themselves inappropriately. This could lead to ridicule, embarrassment, and low self-esteem and can sometimes cause psychological problems in users who are particularly vulnerable. Additionally, Sclater (2008) reports that social networking sites are increasingly subjected to intrusive advertising and that some potential employers are making hiring determinations based on the information presented in a student's private profile.

Mobile Technologies

Mobile wireless technologies are premised on two types of wireless data communication: Short Message Service (SMS) and Wireless Application Protocols (WAP) (also called Wireless Access Points). Mobile wireless technologies include wireless laptop computers, wireless handheld computers (e.g., palmtop and tablet computers), and wireless handheld devices such as cell phones or smart phones (e.g., iPhone), PDAs (e.g., Blackberries), GPS (Global Positioning Systems), and Bluetooth technologies. Motiwalla (2007) refers to mobile technologies as wireless/handheld or W/H. Mobile technologies are now supporting Multimedia Messaging Services (MMS) (through digital cameras, and audio and video downloads), e-mail, instant messaging (e.g., IM), and other types of communication tools such as discussion groups and file-sharing capabilities that users typically access through a Web browser and operating system. For example, users can download Windows Messenger Live (part of Microsoft Online Office Tools) for free to their mobile devices and use it to enable IM.

Mobile technologies are increasingly gaining ground in higher- education contexts and enabling a new type of distributed learning or e-Learning known as mobile learning, m-Learning or ML (Motiwalla, 2007). ML is truly anytime, anywhere learning because it allows maximum physical mobility in addition to Internet access. Several universities have undertaken learning projects that require the use of different mobile wireless technologies and networks (Kim, Mims, & Holmes, 2006). Key uses include providing students with access to information resources, enabling participation in wireless polling during class, enhancing collaboration, offering mobile data-gathering tools to students, and supporting innovative teaching practices.

It is important to note, however, that mobile technologies can also act as distracters, especially for students who have not learned to self-regulate their academic studying very well (Zimmerman, 2002). In an ECAR 2007 study of undergraduate students and information technology, Salaway, Caruso, and Nelson reported that virtually all of the study respondents (27,846 undergraduates) owned some type of mobile device. Specifically, 86.1 percent owned a simple cell phone (not web-enabled), 12 percent owned a smart phone (web-enabled cell phone/PDA), 11.9 percent owned a PDA, 76.4 percent owned an electronic music/video device, and 73.7 percent owned a laptop. Given these statistics, college instructors and faculty must think critically to determine how to use mobile technologies and social software overall to help students achieve educational goals (Kim et al., 2006).

Research on Social Software and Mobile Learning

Overall, empirical research on Web 2.0-enabled social software is limited due to its relative newness. However, several studies have recently been published that provide insight into the benefits of using social software in higher education contexts. According to Ferdig (2007), social software supports social networking among groups or individuals and allows those who participate to engage in conversational interactions and opportunities for social feedback. These conversational interactions can include e-mail, photo-share websites (e.g., Flickr), blogging, and social networks such as Facebook. Ferdig suggests that social software can benefit teacher preparation and education through four channels: (a) scaffolding, by which more knowledgeable professionals can guide students in online forums; (b) collaborative learning, by which LMS such as Blackboard provide opportunities for students to work together; (c) publishing capability, which enables students to produce tangible evidence of their learning and provides them with opportunities for feedback and self-reflection; and (d) involvement in learning communities, where students can exchange ideas and challenge one another.

With regard to mobile learning, Chen, Chang, and Wang (2008) assessed how combining both a mobile learning device (e.g., cell phone) and a ubiquitous learning environment (e.g., learning website) may influence measures of student learning. Three different support systems using mobile learning devices were designed. The first system was the Learning Status Awareness Module (LSAM) that sent students daily messages about which concepts to learn and pop quizzes to provide learning opportunities. The second system was the Schedule Reminder System (SRS), which allowed easy access to class schedules, prompted students on upcoming tasks, and attempted to motivate students to achieve their learning goals. The third system was the Mentor Arrangement Module (MAM), which allowed students to directly contact mentors or other classmates to provide help whenever needed. Additionally, a web-based learning system was developed to complement the mobile learning devices as well as provide additional resources for students to consult. Students who had participated in the mobile learning support systems achieved higher academic ratings and were more likely to accomplish their learning goals than students who did not participate in the mobile learning support systems.

Additionally, Motiwalla (2007) examined 63 students' perceptions of mobile learning enabled by a variety of W/H devices in a higher-education context across two semesters. A prototype of a mobile-learning application was developed to complement classroom or distance learning in undergraduate and graduate courses, and was linked to three course websites. Students reported their experiences through a quantitative Likert-type survey and interviews at the end of each semester. The results revealed that students generally liked the use of W/H devices for learning and perceived them as having a potentially strong role in improving the "flexibility and efficiency" of learning environments (p. 593). Furthermore, more than 60 percent of participants agreed that, overall, mobile learning is a valuable and useful learning tool.

Researchers have also examined the impact of podcasting, an experience- and resource-sharing social software technology, on collaborative learning and knowledge building (Lee, McLoughlin, & Chan, 2008). As described in Chapter 2, podcasts are downloadable audio files available for students who have handheld audio devices. In the Lee et al. study, the podcasts were developed by students nearing the end of an information technology class and were intended to become resources for future students. Developing these podcasts required students to collaborate, develop and plan ideas for discussion, and conceptualize lectures. At the end of the podcasting project, students demonstrated increased knowledge of the course subject matter as well as effective collaborative learning and knowledge-building skills.

A related study by Evans (2008) examined college freshmen's attitudes toward lectures, podcasts, class notes, textbooks, and multimedia e-Learning systems after having students use a series of revision podcasts to help them prepare for the final exam in an Information and Communications Technology (ICT) course. The results indicated that students rated podcasts as more-effective revision tools than their textbooks and as more efficient than their own notes in helping them learn. The results of this study suggest that podcasting may have a significant potential as an innovative learning tool for undergraduates because of its flexible use and effective and efficient information delivery.

These research findings clearly demonstrate that social software use in higher education contexts can lead to improved learning. The question then is, How can instructors like Steve use social software specifically to support student self-regulation? We discuss this next.

Supporting Self-Regulation Using Social Software

As mentioned earlier in this chapter, social software tools have pedagogical affordances that can help support and promote student self-regulation by enabling the creation of personal and social learning environments or experiences (PLE/SLE). In order to demonstrate how instructors can intentionally use social software to scaffold students' self-regulation skills in their courses, we developed a cyclical model of social software use based on the levels of social interactivity that social software tools enable. These levels are: (1) personal information management, (2) social interaction and collaboration, and (3) information aggregation and management.

At level 1, personal information management, instructors can demonstrate to students how social software tools, particularly experience- and resource-sharing tools, and Web and online office tools can be used to create a personal learning environment (PLE) that enables them to begin self-managing course information on their own. Essentially, at this level social software tools are used to scaffold the cognitive processes that the learner undertakes prior to initiating a learning task such as goal setting and time management (see Chapters 4 and 7).

At level 2, social interaction and collaboration, instructors can expose students to communication and social networking tools that foster participation in learning communities surrounding the course topics, and/or to create their own social learning environment (SLE) based on selected topics and interests. Also at this level, the value of the network increases for everyone as more students begin interacting by means of a particular social software tool. Students begin to incorporate the strategies needed to actually perform the learning task using task strategies and self-monitoring, and receiving help and feedback from instructor and peers.

At level 3, information aggregation and management, instructors can encourage students to use experience- and resource-sharing tools to aggregate information from the SLE in order to reflect on their learning experience. At this level, social software tools can enhance the overall process of redistributing, republishing, and remixing content and information. This enables students to engage in self-evaluation and to self-reflect on the social and learning experience in order to make adjustments to the PLE that they created in level 1. Table 10.1 provides examples of social software use at each of these levels.

In essence, this cyclical model of social software use aligns with Zimmerman's (2000) three-phase conceptual model of self-regulated learning presented in Chapter 1. Recall that Zimmerman's model includes the forethought phase, the performance phase, and the self-reflection phase. The forethought phase aligns with level 1 of the social software use model (personal information management), because it is a preliminary phase or level in which the learner prepares for the learning task or activity. The second phase of Zimmerman's model, the performance phase, aligns with level 2 of the social software use model (social interaction and collaboration), because it represents the action phase of self-regulated learning during which the learner employs the strategies to actually perform the learning task within the learning community. The final phase of Zimmerman's model, self-reflection, aligns with level 3 of the social software use model (information aggregation and management), because it is within this phase that the learner evaluates his or her overall learning performance and experience. This evaluation or self-reflection is then utilized by the learner to influence the forethought phase of subsequent efforts, leading the learner to make adjustments to the PLE created in level 1 of the social software use model. Thus the three phases of Zimmerman's model and the three levels of the social software use model are interrelated in a self-oriented system of reflective feedback to support and promote self-regulated learning. The effective self-regulated learner continues to adjust self-regulated strategies using social software tools across the three levels of the social software use model in order to optimize learning and to effectively direct aspects of the learning experience toward a desired outcome.

TABLE 10.1 Supporting Self-Regulated Learning Using Social Software

	(Level 1) Personal information management	(Level 2) Social interaction and collaboration	(Level 3) Information aggregation and management
Experience- and resource-sharing tools	Instructor encourages students to use a blog as a private journal to document course tasks, set learning and assignment goals	Instructor asks students to enable the blog sharing features to allow instructor and peer feedback as well as referencing of blogposts using the blog trackback feature	Instructor demonstrates how to configure a blog to pull in other users' references, posts, comments, or recommended content (e.g., through RSS feeds)
Web or online office tools	Instructor encourages students to use Google Calendar for personal time planning and task management	Instructor asks students to enable the calendar sharing features to allow instructor and peer feedback Instructor asks students to collaboratively use the online calendar for managing team projects, activities, and tasks	Instructor demonstrates how to archive personal and group calendars to enable self-evaluation and self-reflection
Experience- and resource-sharing tools	Instructor encourages students to use Flickr or YouTube to set up a personal media archive related to course content	Instructor asks students to enable the sharing feature of the media archive and join similar media archives created by peers	Instructor demonstrates how to aggregate media from several shared media archives to create a more selective archive based on deeper understanding of related content
Social networking tools	Instructor encourages students to create a personal profile on Facebook or LinkedIn related to their academic and career goals	Instructor encourages students to link to communities and groups related to their professional interests and learning goals and to engage in relevant discussion	Instructor asks students to self-evaluate and reflect on their social network experience Instructor asks students to restructure their profile and social presence accordingly
Experience- and resource-sharing tools	Instructor encourages students to use a social bookmarking tool to organize course content	Instructor encourages students to share their bookmarks with other classmates and to use group tags to enable folksonomic classification of course content	Instructor asks students to restructure their bookmarks and tags after self-evaluating and reflecting on the social learning experience

Conclusion

This chapter has provided an overview of Web 2.0 and social software and a model that can help instructors and faculty adopt new approaches to using ILT in higher-education contexts. It is concluded that educators, faculty, and administrators cannot afford to ignore the power of social media; rather, they need to mindfully embrace it, as demonstrated in the examples provided in this chapter.

References

Alexander, B. (2006). Web 2.0: a new wave of innovation for teaching and learning? *EDUCAUSE Review, 41*(2), 32–44. Retrieved June 13, 2006, from: http://www.educause.edu/ir/library/pdf/ERM0621.pdf

Anderson, P. (2007). What is Web 2.0? Ideas, technologies, and implications for education. *JISC Technology and Standards Watch, February 2007.* Retrieved July 14 2008 from: http://www.jisc.ac.uk/media/documents/techwatch/tsw0701b.pdf

Bianchini, G. (2008). Gina Bianchini: Ning. In B. L. Jones (Ed.), *Interviews with 20 Web 2.0 influencers: Web 2.0 heroes* (pp. 45–54). Indianapolis, IN: Wiley Publishing Inc.

Butterfield, S. (2003, March 24). *An article complaining about 'social software'...* Syllogue Weblog. Retrieved February 10, 2006, from: http://www.sylloge.com/personal/2003_03_01_s.html#91273866

Carroll, D. (2008). Dorion Carroll: Technorati. In B. L. Jones (Ed.), *Interviews with 20 Web 2.0 influencers: Web 2.0 heroes* (pp. 55–78). Indianapolis, IN: Wiley Publishing Inc.

Chen, G. D., Chang, C. K., & Wang, C. Y. (2008). Ubiquitous learning website: Scaffold learners by mobile devices with information-aware techniques. *Computers & Education, 50,* 77–90.

Dabbagh, N. (April 2004). *Using blogs as a teaching and learning tool.* Faculty development presentation at the Instructional Resource Center (IRC) and the Center for Teaching Excellence, George Mason University, Fairfax, Virginia.

Dabbagh, N., & Reo, R. (2010). Back to the future: Tracing the roots and learning affordances of social software. In M. Lee & C. McLoughlin (Eds.), *Web 2.0-based e-learning: Applying social informatics for tertiary teaching.* Hershey, PA: IGI Global.

Davis, M. (2008). *Semantic wave 2008 report: Industry roadmap to Web 3.0 & multi-billion dollar market opportunities (executive summary).* Washington DC: Project 10X. Retrieved June 16, 2008 from: http://www.project10x.com/

EDUCAUSE Learning Initiative (ELI). (2007). *The seven things you need to know about....* Retrieved January 15, 2008 from: http://connect.educause.edu/Library/ELI/7ThingsYouShouldKnowAbout/

Evans, C. (2008). The effectiveness of m-learning in the form of podcast revision lectures in higher education. *Computers & Education, 50*, 491–498.

Ferdig, R. (2007). Editorial: Examining social software in teacher education. *Journal of Technology and Teacher Education, 15*(1), 5–10.

Jones, B. (Ed.). (2008). *Interviews with 20 Web 2.0 influencers: Web 2.0 heroes*. Indianapolis, IN: Wiley.

Kim, S. H., Mims, C., & Holmes, K. P. (2006). An introduction to current trends and benefits of mobile wireless technology use in higher education. *AACE Journal, 14*(1), 77–100.

Lee, M., McLoughlin, C., & Chan, A. (2008). Talk the talk: Learner-generated podcasts as catalysts for knowledge creation. *British Journal of Educational Technology, 39*(3), 501–521.

Lindstrom, P. (2007, April 20). Securing "Web 2.0" technologies. Midvale, Utah: Burton Group. *EDUCAUSE Center for Applied Research*. Retrieved February 3, 2008 from: http://net.educause.edu/ir/library/pdf/ecar_so/ers/ers0703/rs/ERS0703.pdf

Madden, M., & Fox, S. (2006). Riding the waves of "Web 2.0": More than a buzzword, but still not easily defined. *Pew Internet Project*. Retrieved September 1, 2008 from: http://www.pewinternet.org/pdfs/PIP_Web_2.0.pdf

Motiwalla, L.F. (2007). Mobile learning: A framework and evaluation. *Computers & Education, 49*, 581–596.

New Media Consortium & EDUCAUSE Learning Initiative (2007). *The 2007 horizon report*. Retrieved December 14, 2007 from: http://www.nmc.org/pdf/2007_Horizon_Report.pdf

Oravec, J. (2002). Bookmarking the world: Weblog applications in education. *Journal of Adolescent & Adult Literacy, 45*(7), 616–621.

O'Reilly, T. (2005). What is Web 2.0: Design patterns and business models for the next generation of software. *O'Reilly Radar*. Retrieved July 23, 2006 from: http://www.oreillynet.com/pub/a/oreilly/tim/news/2005/09/30/what-is-web-20.html

O'Reilly, T. (December, 2006). Web 2.0 compact definition: Trying again. *O'Reilly Radar*. Retrieved July 12, 2008 from: http://radar.oreilly.com/2006/12/web-20-compact-definition-tryi.html

Salaway, G., Caruso, J., & Nelson, M.R. (2007). The ECAR study of undergraduate students and information technology, 2007. Retrieved March 5, 2008 from: http://connect.educause.edu/Library/ECAR/TheECARStudyofUndergradua/45075

Schachter, J. (2008). Joshua Schachter: del.icio.us. In B. L. Jones (Ed.), *Interviews with 20 Web 2.0 influencers: Web 2.0 heroes* (pp. 169–176). Indianapolis, IN: Wiley Publishing Inc.

Sclater, N. (2008). Web 2.0, personal learning environments, and the future of learning management systems (Research Bulletin, Issue 13). Boulder, CO: EDUCAUSE Center for Applied Research, 2008, available from: http://www.educause.edu/ecar.

Sessum, C. (January, 2006). *Notes on the significance of the emergence of blogs and wikis.* Weblog/Elgg Community Learning Space. Retrieved October 12, 2006 from: http://elgg.net/csessums/weblog/6172.html

Shirky, C. (2003). Work on networks: A GBN tour by Clay Shirky (October 2003). *A GBN (Global Business Network) Report.* Retrieved January 23, 2008 from: http://www.gbn.com/GBNDocumentDisplayServlet.srv?aid=13227 &url=%2FUploadDocumentDisplayServlet.srv%3Fid%3D13976

Stone, B. (2008). Biz Stone: Twitter. In B. L. Jones (Ed.), *Web 2.0 heroes: Interviews with 20 Web 2.0 influencers* (pp. 145–154). Indianapolis, IN: Wiley Publishing Inc.

Zimmerman, B. J. (2000). Attainment of self-regulation: A social cognitive perspective. In M. Boekaerts, P. Pintrich, & M. Zeidner (Eds.), *Self-regulation: Theory, research, and applications* (pp.13–39). Orlando, FL: Academic Press.

Zimmerman, B. J. (2002). Becoming a self-regulated learner: An overview. *Theory Into Practice, 41*(2), 64–70.